LATCH

LATCH

A HANDBOOK FOR BREASTFEEDING
WITH CONFIDENCE AT EVERY STAGE

Robin Kaplan, M.Ed., IBCLC

Foreword by Abby Theuring

ROCKRIDGE PRESS

For general information on our other products and services or to obtain technical support, please contact our Customer Care Department within the United States at (866) 744-2665, or outside the United States at (510) 253-0500.

Rockridge Press publishes its books in a variety of electronic and print formats. Some content that appears in print may not be available in electronic books, and vice versa.

Illustrations © 2018 by Julia Yellow
Cover photography © Image Source/Getty Images

ISBN: Print 978-1-62315-930-6 | eBook 978-1-62315-931-3

For all the new families who are sick of consulting Dr. Google
And to my sons, Ben and Ryan

Contents

Weaning from Breastfeeding 107

Foreword

Breastfeeding is natural, but it is not a cultural norm in the United States. We expect that because it is natural, it will be easy, and that we will somehow know exactly what to do, as will our babies. As a result, many of us go into parenthood with breastfeeding blinders on. We commit our hearts to breastfeeding, but we don't prepare our minds and bodies for how to do it. Congratulations on supporting your decision to breastfeed by educating yourself with this book!

My personal breastfeeding story was almost a very short one. I'd planned to breastfeed since before I'd even gotten pregnant, yet my newborn son had other ideas. Nursing was a struggle, and I felt like my body was broken. When I should have been sleeping, I stayed up searching for answers online. I read mainstream medical websites as well as chat rooms, where the bad information I had already gotten was enthusiastically compounded by more bad information. I felt scared, anxious, and alone. I never realized how little I knew about breastfeeding. The first time I had ever seen a baby breastfeed was in the hospital, when I looked down at my own latched baby.

I learned about lactation consultants and decided to call one. She was calm and reassuring, and she gave me a few tips. When breastfeeding started to work, it felt like magic. The breastfeeding relationship that I'd imagined having with my son finally became a reality.

Breastfeeding had brought me to my knees, but it ultimately became a symbol of my strength. I created The Badass Breastfeeder, an online community, simply to share my story with my friends. But when I made my story public, I was bombarded with responses. Many other women had had the same experience. The community grew rapidly, with moms who'd struggled to get started with breastfeeding due to a lack of reliable information. As a social worker, I felt a calling to use this community to raise awareness about breastfeeding and to share reliable breastfeeding information. My community is now a quarter of a million strong, filled with empowered moms sharing their stories so that their struggles will not be someone else's. I'm thrilled to read a book with the same mission.

Most of us don't have the benefit of working with a lactation consultant until we're already experiencing difficulty with breastfeeding. Yet what you have in this book is the guidance, wisdom, and warmth of a longtime lactation consultant who wants to prepare you before you find yourself in need. Robin's book cuts through all the confusing and contradictory information that abounds online. Here everything is presented in a simple, easy-to-understand manner. You won't get bogged down with page after page of information that you don't need. Instead, *Latch* gives you practical advice to make breastfeeding work the way you want it to, without judgment regarding any decisions you've made for your family.

ABBY THEURING
The Badass Breastfeeder

Introduction

In 2009, I started the San Diego Breastfeeding Center with a very clear intention. I wanted to be the woman who provided new moms with unconditional, nonjudgmental support to help reach their personal breastfeeding goals. By that point, I was an International Board Certified Lactation Consultant. But my professional journey to opening the center had begun years earlier with a very personal breastfeeding struggle.

My son Benjamin was the first grandchild on both sides of the family. After he was born, family members and friends flew in from all around the country to see him. As he was passed from one adult to another, my bald cherub rested soundly in everyone's arms. Yet as soon as it was time to breastfeed, he went from cherub to piranha.

My mom had breastfed my three siblings and me, so I never thought twice about whether I would breastfeed. *Of course I would.* But breastfeeding Ben was so much more difficult than I ever envisioned. He wouldn't latch properly. It was super painful. When he'd start to root and cry, I'd break out into tears. The seemingly nonstop visitors rotating through my hospital room and living room made my breastfeeding challenges all the more demoralizing. I was a wreck.

Four days after Ben was born, our pediatrician asked me how breastfeeding was going. I sobbed in her office and told her I wasn't sure how much longer I could keep trying. I felt like a failure. I asked her why breastfeeding wasn't working for us. She couldn't answer that question but instead of talking to me about alternative options, she handed me a business card. It was for a lactation consultant who would come to my home and help me with breastfeeding. I called the lactation consultant as soon as I left the doctor's office. The next day, an amazing ray of light in the form of a person showed up at my home, providing tips, tricks, and emotional support. She gave me the courage to keep trying for a few more days. I did, and I noticed changes. The latch got better. My cracked nipples started to heal. Ben was calmer. Those few days quickly turned into weeks.

By the time Ben was six weeks old, I felt like I was starting to get the hang of breastfeeding. Then I remembered we had a wedding to go to. Twelve hours away by car. In an open, public space. Panic set in. At our first rest stop, it became apparent that breastfeeding in a hot car, in August, was not going to work. It was time to bite the bullet and try breastfeeding in an air-conditioned restaurant. As I started to get set up, I pulled down my nursing tank. Lo and behold, my kiddo just hopped right on. No fuss, no pain. I stared at him in amazement. We had arrived. It wasn't until this moment that I finally felt like a breastfeeding mother.

My hope is that this book will provide you, an expectant or new breastfeeding mother, with the support, confidence, and education you need to breastfeed. I feel these components are crucial in a mother's ability to reach her breastfeeding goals. While these alone don't guarantee success, without them success can be difficult.

Breastfeeding is an enormous topic, but the basics don't require a long book. Whether a mother breastfeeds in the United States, Zimbabwe, or Brazil, the basic process and stages she goes through are fundamentally the same. Breastfeeding begins with latching an infant to breast but it certainly doesn't end there. This book breaks breastfeeding into stages and walks moms through fundamental instruction, key advice, and much-needed information regarding their most common questions and concerns.

Whatever your personal breastfeeding goals are, I hope that this book helps you make them happen. No conditions, no judgments. You've got this, mama!

Breastfeeding reminds us of the universal truth of abundance; the more we give out, the more we are filled up, and that divine nourishment, the source from which we all draw, is, like a mother's breast, ever full and ever flowing.

—SARAH J. BUCKLEY, MD, AUTHOR OF *GENTLE BIRTH, GENTLE MOTHERING: A DOCTOR'S GUIDE TO NATURAL CHILDBIRTH AND GENTLE EARLY PARENTING CHOICES*

Preparing to Breastfeed

Congratulations on your pregnancy! Becoming a parent is such an exciting, life-changing experience. You have so much to look forward to with the birth of your child. The sweet scent of your baby's breath as he sleeps on your chest. Her first giggle. His first step. Breastfeeding is something that many expectant moms look forward to, but also feel nervous about. This chapter will help you prepare to breastfeed by sharing the things you'll need to know in these last weeks of pregnancy, helping you understand what your body is doing now to prepare to make milk, and explaining how to create your "dream team" of breastfeeding support.

Breastfeeding is such a personal choice, yet everyone seems to have an opinion to share with expectant mothers. *Do you plan to breastfeed? For how long?* And while you may not be sure about these answers, the fact that you purchased this book shows that you want to know more about this topic. You want to make decisions that make the most sense for you and your growing family. While there are many benefits to breastfeeding, ultimately, the choice to breastfeed and for how long is an ongoing conversation that may change over time. The information in this book is here to guide you and help you make the best educated decision for you and your baby.

Why Breastfeed?

Breastfeeding has tremendous benefits for both Baby and Mom. The list goes on and on, but here are some of the key benefits that breastmilk and breastfeeding provide for both of you, right from the time of Baby's birth:

Benefits for Baby

Breastmilk is the natural first food for babies. It provides all the energy and nutrients that an infant needs for the first months of life, and it continues to provide up to half or more of a child's nutritional needs during the second half of the first year, and up to a third during the second year of life.

Breastfeeding reduces the risk of jaundice. Breastmilk acts as a laxative, helping babies pass meconium (first poops) quickly, which lowers their risk of jaundice.

Breastfeeding promotes bonding. Mothers who breastfeed demonstrate enhanced sensitivity during early infancy that may foster later secure attachment. Oxytocin, the love hormone, is released while breastfeeding, promoting bonding between Mom and Baby.

Breastfeeding helps develop mouth and jaw muscles. The mechanics involved in a baby's breastfeeding efforts promote optimal development of the oral cavity.

Breastfeeding reduces the risk of sudden infant death syndrome (SIDS). SIDS occurs in only one out of two thousand live births, peaking between one and four months of age. Breastfed infants may be more easily aroused from sleep than formula-fed infants in the two- to three-month age range. Breastfeeding also delivers antibodies that may help protect infants from infection during the period they are most at risk for SIDS.

Breastfeeding reduces a baby's risk of contracting some illnesses. Breastmilk aids in the development of a baby's immune system and protects against diseases, including ear infections and bacterial meningitis. It also reduces the risk of developing allergies and asthma. Additionally, the risk of lower respiratory tract infections in the first year is reduced by 72 percent in infants breastfed exclusively for more than four months.

Breastfeeding protects against obesity. Protein and total energy intake, as well as the amount of energy metabolized, is higher among formula-fed infants than among those who are breastfed. This increased body weight during the neonatal period, coupled with higher protein intake and weight gain early in life, is positively associated with the development of obesity later in childhood.

Benefits for Mom

Breastfeeding helps stop postpartum bleeding. Oxytocin released during breastfeeding contracts the uterus to stop the bleeding.

Breastfeeding women have lower risks of some diseases. Women who breastfeed have a lowered risk for developing premenopausal breast cancer and ovarian cancer. Also, women who breastfeed longer have lower rates of type 2 diabetes, high blood pressure, and heart disease.

Breastfeeding women can have increased protection against pregnancy. Women who breastfeed fully (frequently day and night) enough to experience lactation amenorrhea (see page 131) are more than 98 percent protected from pregnancy for six months after birth.

Breastfeeding women experience an earlier return to pre-pregnant weight. They can burn up to 500 calories a day while producing milk.

> **JUST THE FACTS**
> Your Montgomery glands, the little bumps on your areola that have gotten larger during pregnancy, secrete the scent of amniotic fluid, which helps your baby know that your breasts are where she can find food.
> —RENEE KAM, IBCLC

Breastfeeding Recommendations

During your pregnancy, it can be very helpful for you and your partner to discuss your breastfeeding goals. If you're not sure where to begin, here are some questions you can ask yourselves to get started:

- How long would you like to breastfeed?
- Do you plan to exclusively breastfeed, or would you like to also offer pumped milk in a bottle?
- What support do you think you might need to help you reach your goal? (See Building Your Breastfeeding Support Dream Team, page 14, for ideas.)

The American Academy of Pediatrics recommends "exclusive breastfeeding for the first six months of a baby's life, followed by breastfeeding in combination with the introduction of complementary foods until at least 12 months of age, and continuation of breastfeeding for as long as mutually desired by mother and baby."

According to the World Health Organization, "review of evidence has shown that, on a population basis, exclusive breastfeeding for 6 months is the optimal way of feeding infants. Thereafter, infants should receive complementary foods with continued breastfeeding up to 2 years of age or beyond."

These official recommendations may or may not mirror your personal breastfeeding goals. You might want to breastfeed for a shorter period of time, or you may want to aim for longer. That is completely up to your family unit. Every drop of breastmilk that your child receives is incredibly beneficial on so many levels, and figuring out your family's goal for breastfeeding duration will make sure that everyone is on the same page. And if you happen to have any challenges along your breastfeeding journey that are keeping you from reaching your breastfeeding goals, your team can help you and even remind you that it's time to reach out for help.

BREASTFEEDING MYTHS

Breastfeeding can be a controversial topic, mostly because there is a lot of misinformation out there. Let's debunk a few of these myths right now!

MYTH #1:

An expectant mother should "rough up" her nipples before the baby is born.

TRUTH: This was the standard recommendation in the '70s and '80s, but we have a lot more knowledge now! "Roughing up" the nipples by rubbing them with a towel is no longer recommended. It has been found that doing so can actually remove the protective substances produced by the breast during pregnancy and afterward. Also, why intentionally cause nipple pain before Baby is born?

MYTH #2:

If a baby loses weight in the first week, it means Mom's milk supply is low.

TRUTH: All babies lose weight after birth; up to 7 to 10 percent of their birth weight is normal. This is so important to know, and often so worrisome to parents, that it's worth repeating: All babies lose weight after birth. Babies should start gaining weight within two to five days after birth, which is also when Mom's fuller milk starts to come in.

Babies should feed every three hours. More frequent feedings mean that Baby is not getting enough.

TRUTH: Infants feed anywhere from 8 to 14 times in 24 hours and sometimes even more during growth spurts. Their tummies are tiny. If Baby is peeing and pooping and gaining weight appropriately, then Baby is getting enough throughout the day.

MYTH #4:

Breastfeeding hurts for the first few weeks.

TRUTH: Breastfeeding is not supposed to hurt. For the first few weeks, nipple tenderness can be normal, as breastfeeding is a lot of stimulation for your nipples throughout the day and night. However, cracking, bleeding, and bruising are your body's way of telling you something needs to be fixed.

How Breastfeeding Works

Breastfeeding is a process of milk production, milk release, and milk transfer. Let's take a look at each of these to better understand each component.

Milk Production

As you may have noticed, your breasts have already started to prepare for breastfeeding throughout your pregnancy. During your first trimester, your breasts may feel sore and tender. This is because your body is producing more of the hormones estrogen and progesterone, causing milk ducts to develop and multiply. You may also experience breast and areola growth. During your second trimester, another hormone called prolactin increases drastically. This increase causes the milk-producing powerhouses known as alveoli to form on the milk ducts. Alveoli look somewhat like grapes on a vine. Your breasts may also feel heavier, and you could start to produce colostrum (see Colostrum: Your First Milk, page 11). These breast changes will continue through your third trimester, as your nipples and areolae continue to darken and enlarge.

Milk Release

Once your baby is born, your milk volume continues to increase and must come out. Milk is released through a series of milk ejections, or "letdowns." As the baby suckles, her tongue stimulates Mom's nipple, which sends a message to Mom's brain, triggering the alveoli (those milk duct "grapes") to contract and squeeze out the milk. The milk then travels down the milk ducts (the "grapevine") and out of your nipple openings. The pressure created by Baby's suckling keeps milk flowing from one letdown to the next.

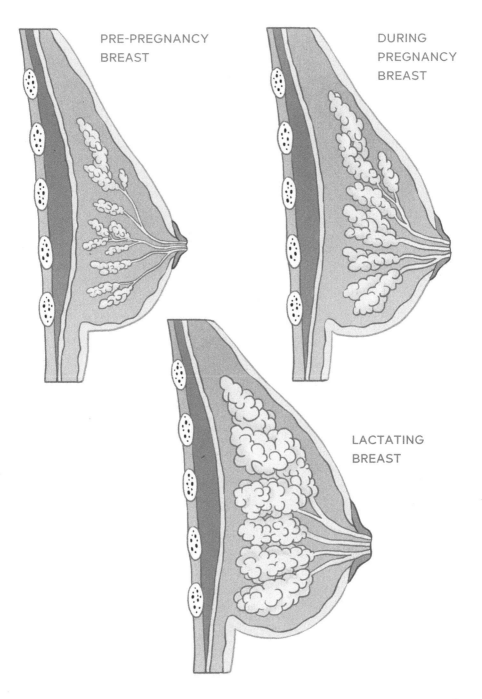

PRE-PREGNANCY
BREAST

DURING
PREGNANCY
BREAST

LACTATING
BREAST

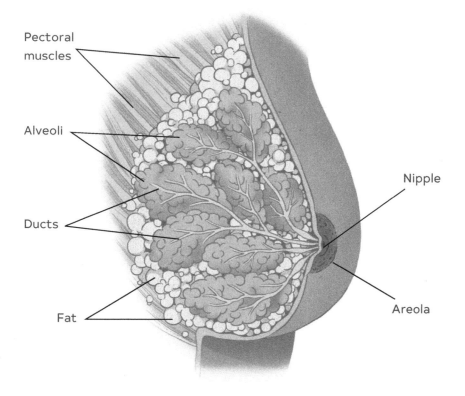

Pectoral
muscles

Alveoli

Ducts

Fat

Nipple

Areola

Milk Transfer

Milk transfer is the act of milk moving from Mom's breast into Baby's mouth and then being swallowed. The baby must continue to suckle during and in between letdowns to keep milk continually flowing. Otherwise, he may either become frustrated with the slow milk flow or just fall asleep doing nonnutritive sucking (sucking without creating enough suction to pull milk out). Milk removal

COLOSTRUM:
YOUR FIRST MILK

Your body has been producing this liquid since your second trimester. Gold in color, thick and viscous in texture, this sticky liquid is the first type of milk your baby will receive from you while breastfeeding. Despite its scant quantity, its quality is jam-packed with nutrients and tons of antibodies for your little newborn. It is super easy to digest and acts as a laxative to help push all of that meconium (Baby's first poops) out of his body, which plays a role in preventing jaundice. Colostrum also helps seal up your baby's gut, preventing foreign substances from penetrating his digestive system as well as helping him kick-start his own immune system. Yeah, it is a pretty amazing liquid! After just a few days, though, your colostrum will transition to mature milk, which is more white in color and thinner and smoother in texture.

and transfer are critical for initiating and maintaining Mom's milk supply, as the more the breasts are emptied, the more Mom's body is told to make more milk. For effective milk transfer, the baby needs to have a deep latch (see page 32) to create enough negative pressure inside his mouth while sucking to remove Mom's milk. Sounds complicated, but how cool that he intuitively knows just what to do!

The Importance of the Latch

The word *latch* refers to the baby's positioning on the mother's breast. Getting a proper latch is essential for both Baby and Mom. The better the latch, the more effectively Baby will be able to remove milk from Mom's breasts. And a great latch will help Mom breastfeed without pain. An improper latch can lead to significant nipple pain, cracked nipples, and plugged ducts. But getting a great latch doesn't have to be complicated. Here are a few steps to achieve a comfortable latch:

1. Bring your baby's body snug to your torso, so that her stomach is facing and touching yours.

2. Line your nipple up with your baby's nose.

3. Tickle your baby with your nipple, starting from her nose and drawing it down to her chin. This will stimulate a reflex, causing her to open her mouth.

4. Tilt your baby's head back slightly, away from your breast, so she is resting her chin on your areola. This will help her open her mouth even more widely as she then leans forward to latch on to your areola and nipple.

The top illustration on the opposite page shows what this good latch looks like. The lower illustration highlights differences that could lead to a poor latch, from the mom's hand placement behind the baby's head to the angling of the baby's forehead and chin, which affects how widely she can open her mouth. Baby's mouth is also very narrow, causing a shallow attachment to the mom's nipple, rather than wider attachment on her areola.

In the next chapter, you will learn more about combining the latch with different breastfeeding positions. If you find that you are having difficulties with latching or positioning your baby, seek additional breastfeeding support as soon as you can.

GOOD LATCH

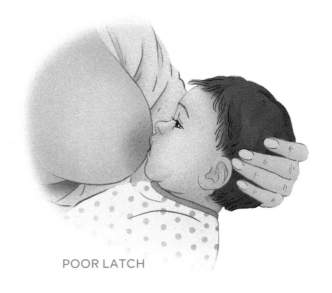

POOR LATCH

Building Your Breastfeeding Support Dream Team

Breastfeeding support has been shown to be the largest indicator of a mother's breastfeeding success—perhaps a surprising statistic for such an intimate experience. One of my favorite recommendations for expectant mothers is to create a personal "dream team of breastfeeding support." So, who should be on your dream team?

Your Partner

If breastfeeding is important to you, then it should be important to your partner, as well. Your partner will need to be your cheerleader, your confidant, and your number-one support person. Your partner will make sure you are well fed and hydrated while you feed and hydrate your baby. Your partner can assist with latching if you need help, as well as call in other support when needed. Your partner can bond with both you and Baby as you breastfeed, nap, eat, and learn to maneuver this new time in your lives. When your partner is on board, you are a united force, working together toward a shared goal, which can feel absolutely empowering!

Mama Tribe

Did your best friend breastfeed? Your sister-in-law? What about a coworker? Don't be hesitant to reach out to others who have breastfed. These pro-breastfeeding friends and family will make up your mama tribe. When you're tired, feeling overwhelmed, or just need someone to give you a hug and tell you everything is going to be just fine, this is a group you can call upon. The women in this group have been there before, have experienced the ups and downs of breastfeeding, and will encourage you to keep on keeping on (as long as you want to). They will support you, bring you food, and help you feel confident. These ladies ROCK!

Breastfeeding-Friendly Pediatrician

If you've been researching other important topics during your pregnancy, you know that you'll need to find a pediatrician for your baby before you deliver. As long as you'll be interviewing a pediatrician or three, try to figure out how much each one can help you with your breastfeeding goals. Some pediatricians are much more well versed in breastfeeding than others. They know how much breastmilk a baby needs per feeding, how much weight a baby should gain per week, how often a baby should be feeding, the difference between nipple tenderness and pain, and when to refer to a lactation consultant, if necessary. Other pediatricians are not likely to sabotage your breastfeeding efforts on purpose, but their own lack of knowledge might lead them to dispense advice that doesn't help you establish your milk supply or the breastfeeding relationship. As a result, they ultimately make things more challenging for Mom and Baby. Ask your friends and post on social media for recommendations. Ask a local international board-certified lactation consultant (IBCLC). You'll be glad you did! Here are a few questions you can ask to vet how breastfeeding-friendly a pediatrician is:

- How long do you think I should breastfeed?
- What are your recommendations if I encounter breastfeeding challenges?
- Can you recommend any local breastfeeding support groups and lactation consultants I can contact if I need help?

Moms' Groups

There are so many types of groups for moms. Breastfeeding support groups, postpartum groups, online Facebook groups, and play-groups can be incredibly supportive when it comes to breastfeeding, among other things. You don't need to attend multiple moms' groups, of course, but do consider joining one. A breastfeeding support group, if offered in your area, can be especially helpful. Many of us are not surrounded by breastfeeding, so we might have no idea what it really looks like or what to expect. At a support group, you can meet other new moms, ask questions, and get a sense of the many ways that women latch their babies. It's awesome!

Moms in these groups aren't reflecting on and remembering their experiences like some of your friends and family might be. They will be in the thick of it, just like you, which really helps build rich and rewarding connections.

Breastfeeding Professional

While books can be helpful in preparing to breastfeed and finding answers to common questions, enlisting the help of a professional, such as a lactation consultant, can be critical if you are having difficulties beyond basic positioning and latching. If your baby takes to breastfeeding quickly and easily, then you will not need a professional on your dream team. But for those who struggle, meeting with someone who has been trained to help others breastfeed can make all the difference in building your confidence and giving you great tools to breastfeed successfully.

Many types of professionals and volunteers can help with breastfeeding. I always advise expectant mothers to research which support professionals are in their area so they already have a list of those who can help with breastfeeding if needed. Some professional services are currently covered by the Afordable Care Act,

A Mom's Story
STEPHANIE

It has truly taken a village to help me be successful in nursing both of my babies! I knew I wanted to breastfeed, but after the birth of my first son, my passion and commitment to it were a surprise to even me. Tongue ties, lip ties, low weight gain, low supply, poor latch, pain/cracking/bleeding, overactive letdown, and more were all hurdles we had to cross. There is absolutely no way I could have made it to 13 months with my first son and still be going strong at six months with my second without these amazing people:

MY HUSBAND! My passion and commitment to breastfeed my babies surprised him also, but he never questioned it and stood by me no matter what decision I made. He came to appointments, helped get the baby latched on time after time, stood up for me when others questioned why I didn't just quit, and let me cry when it all just became too much. He has truly been my rock through all of this.

MY LACTATION CONSULTANTS! Four different lactation consultants have come alongside me and my babies in our journey together. Every single one encouraged me that I could do it when the hurdles seemed insurmountable. They provided help, advice, referrals, and life-changing solutions that kept us going.

MY TRIBE OF OTHER BREASTFEEDING MAMAS! Friends I have known since childhood, friends I've made in recent years, and people I met through the breastfeeding process made it all possible—some experienced breastfeeding challenges, some didn't have trouble at all, some visited, others called, and one even created an online community to connect us all. These mamas always "got it." They knew why I couldn't quit, why no challenge was too big.

MY BABIES! Even from the very start and even in the face of all of our challenges, my babies have always loved nursing. They didn't quit, so there was no way I could!

SUPPORTING MATERIALS

While a new mom needs only her breasts and a baby to breastfeed, there is a small handful of supporting items you might consider registering for to set yourself up for comfortable breastfeeding:

NURSING BRA   For the first few weeks, you'll probably live in a comfortable, underwire-free nursing bra. Choose one based on your bra size while pregnant and one that stretches so that it can handle the temporary engorgement that may happen around three to five days postpartum. After you've been breastfeeding for a few weeks, your breasts will calm down and you can get fitted for a few really nice, comfortable nursing bras.

NURSING TANK   These amazing contraptions have straps that pull down easily for breastfeeding but keep the rest of your tummy and back covered. Genius! These were my favorite tops to wear when nursing in public, as well.

NURSING PADS   Some moms leak; some don't. You won't know which category you fall into until your milk comes in. You can choose either disposable nursing pads or soft cotton or bamboo reusable nursing pads.

NIPPLE CREAM   Think of this as "nipple ChapStick." Similar to expressed breastmilk, these creams can keep your nipples from getting dry and chapped. You can go with something as basic as organic coconut oil or choose a product made specifically for breastfeeding nipples. No need to wipe these creams off before feeding.

BREASTFEEDING PILLOW   Some moms love breastfeeding pillows for the support they can provide with certain breast-feeding positions, like the Cradle Hold (page 35) and the Football/Clutch (page 37). Other moms find that they lean over too much while using them, so they end up just using a laid-back breastfeeding position without a pillow.

NURSING COVER   For moms who feel nervous or anxious about breastfeeding in front of others, a nursing cover can provide a way to breastfeed without others seeing what they are doing. Most young babies don't mind breastfeeding under a nursing cover. As babies get older, they may prefer to breastfeed in a carrier or wrap, which can also provide some privacy.

PUMP   At the time this book was written, according to the Affordable Care Act, "your health insurance plan must cover the cost of a breast pump. It may be either a rental unit or a new one you'll keep. Your plan may have guidelines on whether the covered pump is manual or electric, the length of the rental, and when you'll receive it (before or after birth)." In the rare instance that your insurance doesn't cover a pump, a double electric pump is great for moms who need to pump more than once a day, and a manual pump is usually fine just for occasional pumping.

some are free, and some have a cost. Each professional has different qualifications, so here's a breakdown of those qualifications as well as whether or not there is a fee for services:

IBCLC: An IBCLC is a health care professional who specializes in the clinical management of breastfeeding. IBCLCs must complete between 300 and 1,000 hours of clinical experience with breastfeeding mothers in addition to over 100 hours of education and a board exam or recertification every five years. This is the person you call when you need more than positioning help. Some reasons for needing an IBCLC might include Baby not gaining weight well, low milk supply or oversupply, damaged nipples, breastfeeding a premature baby or twins, breastfeeding a tongue-tied baby, Baby not feeding effectively, and so on. At the time this book was written, according to the Affordable Care Act, "[federal] guidelines provide for coverage of comprehensive prenatal and postnatal lactation support, counseling, and equipment rental as part of their preventive service recommendations, including lactation counseling."

Lactation educator/counselor: These counselors attended a class about breastfeeding for 20 to 45 hours and took an exam. Their scope of practice allows them to run breastfeeding support groups, teach breastfeeding classes, and provide general breastfeeding support but does not allow them to provide hands-on, individualized breastfeeding guidance. There might be a fee to take one of their classes.

La Leche League (LLL) leader: LLL leaders are volunteers who have breastfed for at least nine months, completed readings and writing exercises, and led groups under supervision of another LLL leader. They can provide general support in a group setting, by phone, and sometimes through in-home visits. LLL leaders refer to IBCLCs if a breastfeeding situation is beyond the scope of normal breastfeeding challenges. Guidance from an LLL leader is free.

NUTRITION BEFORE DELIVERY

You are growing a baby inside you! Can you believe that? So, naturally, what you eat affects not only your health and stamina but also your baby's development. Optimal fetal development is dependent upon a lot of key nutrients, for example folate in the first trimester to prevent spina bifida, and vitamin D and calcium to help Baby build strong bones in the third trimester.

Taking a high-quality multivitamin will guarantee that you meet the recommended amount of nutrients to help grow a healthy baby. Not all prenatal vitamins are created equal. Many contain synthetic vitamins made in a lab, which don't offer the prime benefits of natural vitamins. For optimal health for you and your baby, try to choose a prenatal vitamin with ingredients that come from nature and are whole foods themselves. For example, when looking for a prenatal vitamin, you should see the ingredients folate or methylfolate, and not folic acid, as well as vitamin D_3 instead of D_2. Plus, you can continue to take this prenatal vitamin the entire time you are breastfeeding. In the next chapter, we'll explore foods and supplements that help create and maintain a robust milk supply.

Breastfeeding USA counselor: Breastfeeding USA counselors are volunteers who have breastfed for at least one year and have completed a breastfeeding management course with counseling skills. They provide peer support in person and on the phone and refer to IBCLCs in complex situations. Guidance from a Breastfeeding USA counselor is free.

WIC (Women, Infants, and Children) peer counselor: A WIC employee who has breastfed for at least six months, is or was a WIC participant, and has completed a 20- to 45-hour class on breastfeeding and human lactation can provide breastfeeding support in the WIC setting. This counselor can also teach breastfeeding classes and run breastfeeding support groups. WIC peer counselors should refer to IBCLCs when a breastfeeding challenge is beyond normal. Guidance from a WIC peer counselor is free for WIC participants.

Postpartum doula: Might you hire a birth doula to assist with your delivery? Find out if she or he is a postpartum doula, too. Postpartum doulas help with everything. Many will cook you dinner, clean your home, and offer baby care tips. Some postpartum doulas have taken breastfeeding classes and some have not, so it's a good idea to ask. If your doula is not an IBCLC, she or he should refer you to one in case of significant breastfeeding challenges. There is a fee associated with hiring a postpartum doula.

Frequently Asked Questions

I'M READING THIS BOOK. SHOULD I ALSO ATTEND A PRENATAL BREASTFEEDING CLASS?

Yes! These classes are offered at hospitals, birth centers, community learning spaces, WIC, doctors' offices, and more, and are often free or offered at minimal cost. This is the best place to learn the breastfeeding basics. Sure, you will learn a lot from what's covered in this book, but it is always wonderful to have an instructor in front of you who can answer your questions. Bring your partner with you, too. It's smart to have another set of eyes and ears when learning about this important topic.

MY BREASTS ARE VERY SMALL. CAN I STILL BREASTFEED?

Absolutely! Breast size determines breastmilk capacity, so women with smaller breasts sometimes have to feed their babies more frequently than those with larger breasts, but there are very few women who are unable to breastfeed because of breast size.

IS IT TRUE THAT BREASTFED BABIES DON'T SLEEP THROUGH THE NIGHT?

Not at all! Whether you breastfeed or bottle-feed, your baby's age, temperament, and development will determine how long your baby can sleep uninterrupted.

I AM PREGNANT WITH TWINS. HOW CAN MY BODY POSSIBLY PRODUCE ENOUGH MILK FOR THEM BOTH?

When you breastfeed twins, your breasts will also be getting double the stimulation. Milk supply is based on supply and demand. The greater the demand (that is, the more frequent stimulation and emptying of your breasts), the more your milk supply will increase. Getting lactation guidance soon after birth, especially if your twins are born early, will help you bring in a full milk supply for your babies.

I'M TAKING PRESCRIPTION DRUGS FOR DEPRESSION. WILL THIS AFFECT MY BREASTMILK?

Antidepressant medications will pass through the breastmilk to your baby, but often at much lower rates than during in utero exposure. While there are some risks to taking antidepressants while breastfeeding, the risk of untreated depression can be much greater. Talk with your doctor about your medications to see if they are considered safe to take while breastfeeding.

Establishing Breastfeeding

Breastfeeding is important for public health, but a mother's postpartum emotional health may hinge on the support she receives in her early days with her new baby.

—INTERNATIONAL DOULA INSTITUTE

STAGE 1

The First Two Weeks

. . . .

The day has arrived—you are finally going to meet your little one! There are no words to describe the moment your new baby is placed into your arms. I still get chills thinking about those first few hours after my sons were born. It's like you have been waiting your entire life to meet this little person, and it is almost surreal that you are now holding him on your chest, feeling him breathe, and smelling that amazing newborn scent.

Those first few hours after birth are truly magical. Your body produced birth endorphins, so this is the most alert your newborn will be for the next few days. This is an amazing time to initiate your first breastfeeding encounter. Babies are often drawn to the breast by the scent of the amniotic fluid that your nipples emit. If that isn't amazing enough, holding your baby skin-to-skin also helps stabilize her heart rate, regulates her temperature, encourages her to breathe more regularly, and neurologically centers her. This skin-to-skin contact also benefits Mom by increasing bonding moments and helps

A Mom's Story
DAWN

In early 2012, we received good news: We were expecting! I did my best to set everything up for a different birthing experience than I had for my first child, which resulted in a cesarean delivery. It wasn't until closer to my due date that I was informed I couldn't have a vaginal birth because of my minor heart issue as well as my age. I may have lost that battle, but I was going to do everything in my power to have skin-to-skin with my little girl. I was aware of the evidence-based research on the benefits of skin-to-skin and its success rate with cesarean births. I talked to my pediatrician about this, and he agreed.

The day of my cesarean, my regular pediatrician was out of town, and his replacement wasn't comfortable at all with our skin-to-skin request. Even the director of the family birth center was opposed to our request. The hospital's head labor and delivery nurse helped us get to a compromise—she was my angel! She proposed that if everything looked good, my little girl would be immediately placed on my chest, without any other intrusion.

Because my baby was coming four weeks early, I wasn't sure we would even get the option of skin-to-skin, but our little girl emerged perfectly! When Beth was placed on my chest and covered with a warming blanket, I was in awe. After a little while, she actually scooted and rooted for my breasts and eventually latched and nursed! I just didn't think I would get that experience since she was early. The remembrance still makes me cry. I was so happy I had the team in my corner and the hospital went forward with my wishes. Beth breastfed for 28 months. We have such a connection, and I attribute it to the wonderful team that helped me get skin-to-skin in the OR! Since my experience, the hospital team has persevered in getting the post-cesarean skin-to-skin policy changed at the hospital!

to bring in your milk supply. Basically, skin-to-skin is one of the best ways to soothe your baby, and it's so intimate, so why not start from her first moment of life? Partners can also take part in skin-to-skin, although it won't help bring in their milk supply (bummer!).

If you and your baby happen to be separated after birth, finding time for skin-to-skin as soon as possible will benefit both of you.

The Birth Day

As soon as your baby is born, assuming it is an uncomplicated birth and your baby is healthy and can remain with you, she will immediately be placed on your chest or in your arms so that you can start enjoying skin-to-skin. Take advantage of your baby's alertness within those first two hours after birth by attempting to latch her. Babies then become pretty sleepy for the rest of the first 24 hours, so you might have to wake your baby every two to three hours to initiate breastfeeding that first day. Be prepared, however, for your soundly sleeping one-day-old will most likely wake up like a starving hibernating bear at 24 hours!

If your baby wants to feed more frequently than every two to three hours, that's totally normal for the first day and into the first few weeks, as it is Baby's job to bring in your milk supply by feeding frequently. In fact, putting a baby to the breast in response to any hunger cues is excellent for bringing in a full milk supply. Babies tend to breastfeed anywhere from 20 to 40 minutes at a time, spending time on both breasts during each feeding session.

Feel free to hold your baby as much as you can! This might seem like a silly comment, yet you will most likely read on the Internet that you shouldn't let your baby sleep in your arms because, they say, you could spoil her. "She will never fall asleep on her own!" they will tell you. This is absolutely not true. Babies need to be held in order to form attachment and feel secure. She just spent nine months growing in your warm, quiet, limited-space abdomen.

A WORD ON JAUNDICE

Jaundice is a common issue to be aware of but not worry over. Throughout your pregnancy, your baby had extra red blood cells to carry oxygen from your body. After birth, these extra red blood cells are no longer needed, so your baby's liver breaks them down, sending bilirubin into his blood stream. Your colostrum, a diuretic and laxative, helps him excrete the bilirubin in a timely manner—usually within the first few days.

Some babies are more prone to higher levels of bilirubin, such as premature babies, babies delivered by vacuum or forceps, and those with blood incompatibility with Mom and genetic predispositions. If Baby becomes jaundiced, his skin and eyes appear yellowish, and he might become much more sleepy and difficult to feed. If your baby has slightly elevated bilirubin levels, it's helpful to breastfeed more frequently to get him to pee and poop a bit more. Sometimes it is recommended to offer a supplement, such as pumped milk or formula, to speed this process. If Baby's jaundice levels get too high, he might need photo-therapy (which looks like a tanning bed) and daily blood work to monitor his bilirubin levels. If your baby is jaundiced, it might feel like a temporary setback to exclusive breastfeeding. At this time, just make sure your baby is feeding effectively and that your milk supply is coming in as needed. Essentially, the sooner that Baby poops out the bilirubin, the sooner this hurdle will be cleared.

The bright, loud, spacious, chaotic world outside your womb can feel very overwhelming, so there is nothing more soothing to her than sleeping in your arms. So embrace it! You will end up with a calmer, better-rested infant, which benefits everyone, right? And, yes, Baby will eventually sleep on her own, I promise!

Shots, Tests, and Screenings

In the first few hours to days after birth, your baby will also get a few shots, tests, and screenings. The typical hospital infant exam includes a vitamin K shot, erythromycin eye ointment, newborn screening tests, a hepatitis B shot, and a hearing screening, as well as a first bath. Home birth looks similar, but with no hepatitis B shot, hearing screening, and newborn bath.

Blood sugar levels will also be tested at a home birth if your baby is showing signs of low blood sugar. Hospitals routinely test blood sugar levels for babies who are at risk for neonatal hypoglycemia; these include babies small for gestational age (SGA), large for gestational age (LGA), born to mothers who have diabetes, or who are late preterm. If your baby's glucose levels are too low, you might be asked to start pumping colostrum to offer to your baby, in addition to breastfeeding every two hours. If colostrum is not available, ask if your hospital has pasteurized donor milk to supplement with until you are able to produce more colostrum.

> JUST THE FACTS
> Your milk jump-starts your baby's immune system. Your milk contains healthy bacteria, antibodies, white blood cells, antimicrobials, and cell wall protectors, which is the science behind why exclusively breastfed babies have a significantly lower risk of contracting infections.
> —BREASTFEEDING MEDICINE

The First Breastfeeding Encounter

As a new mom, that first breastfeeding session may feel so natural, or it might feel intimidating. This is understandable—it's not like you're able to practice this beforehand! No matter where you deliver, your midwife, attending nurses, or birth doula can often help with that first positioning and latch. If you feel like you could use some assistance, just ask! These professionals can show you how to place your baby in your arms, line your baby up for optimal positioning (aligning your nipple to Baby's nose), and ensure a deep latch for maximum comfort. If this is at all painful, ask for help to reposition your baby, and possibly request a visit from a lactation consultant as soon as possible.

For Baby's first feeding and for the next few days, he will be getting colostrum, your first milk (see page 11). Don't worry about quantity—the amount of colostrum your baby needs at each feeding is about 5 to 7 milliliters—that's about a teaspoon! If you have breastfed before, your colostrum might be a bit more abundant, especially if you are still nursing an older child. Regardless, this minimal amount is all your baby needs to satisfy his hunger and thirst for the first 24 hours.

Breastfeeding Positions

You can try several different breastfeeding positions in order to determine which is most comfortable for you and your baby. Some babies are able to just latch on to the breast without any assistance from Mom. Other babies need some guidance in the beginning. You can help your baby place her head in the perfect position and compress your breast into a "breast sandwich" (as shown on the opposite page) so it's easier to latch onto. To make a breast sandwich, think of what you would do when trying to bite into an enormous double-decker sandwich that was too tall to fit into your

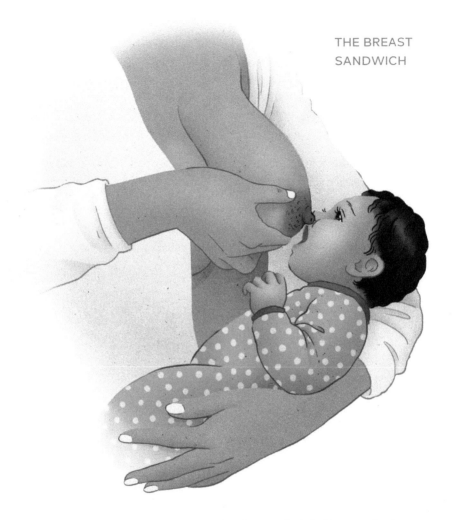

mouth—you'd press down to make the sandwich flatter! The breast
sandwich is the same concept; you're compressing your areola so
it lines up with your baby's mouth, making it so Baby can get more
breast tissue into her mouth when latching. To go with that sandwich, here are some typical breastfeeding positions:

Laid-Back Hold

This is my favorite position because it uses a baby's innate latching reflexes, it doesn't require extra pillows, and it can be done anywhere. Babies tend to feel more secure and stable when prone (lying on their tummies). This way, gravity is pulling your baby onto you while helping her drop her jaw for a wider latch. Here's how:

1. Lean back like you are slouching on your couch, watching TV. Maybe cross your legs to feel more comfortable.

2. Bring your baby onto your chest, with her whole body turned toward yours. She can lie vertically, diagonally (as shown here), horizontally—the positions are endless!

3. Rest Baby's head on your bicep, and let her attempt to latch on her own.

4. If she needs some help latching, cup your breast to hold it in place and create the breast sandwich.

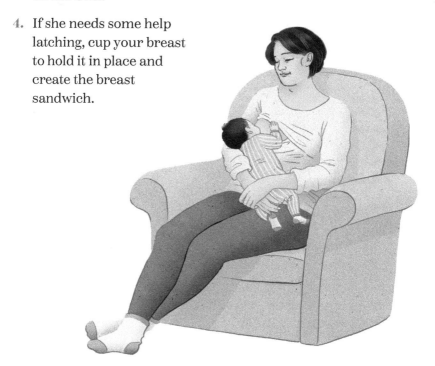

Cradle Hold

This position can be done with or without a breastfeeding pillow.

1. Turn your baby's torso toward yours so that he is completely facing your breast.

2. Rest Baby's head in the crook of your arm, running your arm along his back to provide support.

3. Aim your nipple for his nose, and tuck him in close to help him latch on.

Cross-Cradle Hold

This position can be done with or without a breastfeeding pillow and can be especially helpful for young babies who need a little bit more guidance from you when latching.

1. Turn your baby's torso toward yours so that she is completely facing you.

2. Bring your arm (the one that is opposite of the breast your baby is latching onto) along Baby's back, resting your hand along her shoulder blades and neck.

3. Use your other hand to hold your breast as you bring Baby to your breast, nose toward your nipple.

4. As soon as Baby's chin makes contact with your breast, she will tilt her head back and open widely so you can gently guide her to latch.

Football/Clutch Hold

This is a great position after a cesarean birth, as it keeps Baby off your tender abdomen. You'll need some pillows along your side to provide support for your arm when holding your baby.

1. Pivot your baby so that his belly is touching the side of your body.

2. Bring your arm along Baby's back, resting your hand along his shoulder blades and neck.

3. Aim your nipple for his nose, and tuck him in close to help him latch on.

Side-Lying Hold

This is a fantastic position to master so you can get some rest while breastfeeding.

1. Lie on your side with your baby facing you, lying on his side.

2. Tuck your bottom arm back behind your head, to create some extra space around your breast for Baby's head.

3. Aim your nipple for his nose, and tuck him in close to you, with your top hand pressed along his back to help him latch on.

4. Once he's latched, you can place a rolled-up blanket or pillow behind him to provide gentle support and keep him from rolling away from your breast while feeding.

BREASTFEEDING A PREEMIE

There are more than 500,000 preterm births annually in the United States, 350,000 of which are late preterm (34 to 37 weeks gestation). Babies born before 37 weeks are at a higher risk for temporary breastfeeding difficulties, as they have low energy stores, tend to be fairly sleepy, and often have uncoordinated oral-motor movements. They also tend to be super inconsistent, sometimes feeding well and other times being too sleepy to eat. How quickly your baby demonstrates that she is a coordinated feeder will determine when she will go home with you. When a preterm baby is healthy and feeding well, you will want to monitor her weight every week until her due date, just to confirm that she is gaining appropriately.

If your preterm baby goes to the NICU, this is not a dealbreaker for breastfeeding. If she is able to breastfeed while there, offer your breast as often as you can. Sometimes a nipple shield can be helpful for latching small preterm babies. If your baby needs supplementation, ask the nurses or IBCLC to show you how to pump and offer ways to supplement your baby in the most breastfeeding-friendly way possible. Some recommendations might include finger-feeding (see page 131) and supplementing at the breast rather than just going straight to the bottle (which also is not a dealbreaker for breastfeeding). If your baby needs supplementation due to temporary breastfeeding difficulties, you will want to pump every three hours to bring in your milk supply and keep it going until she is able to start breastfeeding more easily. If breastfeeding your preterm baby is a challenge, think of this as a temporary hurdle and ask for help every day. If it is still a challenge once you are home, reach out to an IBCLC for additional assistance.

Breastfeeding Multiples

Breastfeeding multiples is absolutely possible! Some moms prefer to tandem nurse (breastfeed both babies at the same time). Others prefer to breastfeed one baby at a time, back to back. Others alternate breastfeeding and bottle-feeding. Or you can mix it up and use all three scenarios depending on time of day, location, and so on. How you breastfeed your multiples will be determined in part by your babies' gestational age (see Breastfeeding a Preemie, page 39), how effective they are at breastfeeding, your comfort level, and your personal breastfeeding goals. If breastfeeding is going well, tandem nursing can be a great time-saver and can be done in a variety of positions. On the next two pages, you'll find illustrations of the sidelying position for twins, double cradle hold, same direction hold, and double football hold.

Here are some great tricks for tandem nursing:

- Invest in a twin breastfeeding pillow. It is sturdier and wider than pillows for singletons and will provide you the needed body support for latching two kiddos at the same time.
- When one baby wakes to breastfeed, awaken the other so both can feed at the same time.
- Props are awesome! A bouncy chair can serve as a holding station while you latch the first baby. Rolled-up receiving blankets can be placed behind the babies once they are latched, allowing you to breastfeed hands-free as well as provide support for one baby if the other baby unlatches and needs some assistance in relatching.
- Search YouTube for videos on tandem nursing, as the visuals can be very helpful.

DOUBLESIDE-LYING

DOUBLE CRADLE HOLD

SAME DIRECTION HOLD

DOUBLE
FOOTBALL HOLD

LATCH

BABY BONDING BEYOND THE BREAST

Breastfeeding is an extraordinary way to bond with your baby, but there are also many other ways that both you and your partner can connect and find closeness with your baby. The bonding experience can help build confidence for you as new parents. Bonding with your baby doesn't just have to involve feeding but instead can center around merely providing comfort and attachment. Your partner can bond by bathing the baby, letting the baby sleep on his or her chest, and wearing the baby in a carrier, wrap, or sling. A partner can soothe a fussy baby by bouncing on an exercise ball, taking her on a walk, rocking her, singing or talking to her, cuddling her, and spending time skin-to-skin. When your partner relaxes with you while you are breastfeeding, this also fosters bonding and intimacy among the three of you as a new family unit, and between the two of you as you grow as new parents together.

You may also want to find alternate ways to bond with Baby other than breastfeeding, especially if breastfeeding is temporarily challenging. Breastfeeding takes up a good part of the day, so simply resting with your little one and spending time holding her when not feeding (in addition to the aforementioned tips) can help build priceless closeness and connection.

Getting as Much Help as You Can

Statistics show that a very large percentage of moms start breast-feeding immediately after birth. Unfortunately, that number drops drastically within the first few days and continues to plummet within the first three months. But this drop in breastfeeding rates is not due to a lack of desire to breastfeed! Instead, it is caused by a lack of breastfeeding support for moms, which can lead to personal frustrations, concerns for the baby, and a general lack of confidence in one's own ability to nurse. While breastfeeding can pose challenges, if a mother receives gentle, kind, and ongoing support, she is much more likely to succeed.

After your baby is born, soak up as much assistance and information as you can from the nurses, lactation consultants, and midwives or doctors—that's what they are there for. The sooner you get help, the sooner you will overcome any breastfeeding challenges and get closer to meeting your personal breastfeeding goals.

If You Need to Pump

Typically, it is not recommended to start pumping until a few weeks after your baby is born; however, sometimes extenuating circumstances prompt the need to pump early on. You might be encouraged to pump early if your baby

- is in the neonatal intensive care unit (NICU).
- will not latch.
- experiences excessive weight loss (more than 10 percent of birth weight).
- has elevated jaundice levels.
- has caused significant damage to your nipples.

If your baby is not physically with you to bring in your milk supply, your pump can attempt to do it for you. Even if your newborn

THE STAGES OF BREASTMILK

Your milk goes through a few transitions after your baby is born. As mentioned, your body begins to make colostrum during your first trimester. This thick, viscous first milk after birth is packed with nutrients and immunological properties. Colostrum is very low in volume those first few days (5 milliliters per feeding the first day to about 30 milliliters per feeding on Day 3), so its nutrients are very concentrated. It also works as a laxative to help your baby poop out all of the meconium (Baby's first few stools). By Days 3 to 5 postpartum, your milk will start to look more white in color as it transitions from colostrum to mature milk. Your breasts will also feel fuller and heavier as your milk volume increases. The volume will continue to increase each day until your baby is about two weeks old and then plateau, unless your milk supply needs some extra assistance in increasing to meet your baby's need.

is being finger-fed or bottle-fed, this doesn't mean that you won't be able to eventually breastfeed.

Just remember the two general "rules" of feeding a baby. Rule #1 is to feed the baby. Rule #2, for breastfeeding mothers, is to protect your milk supply—and this is where pumping can help. A lactation consultant can assist with reestablishing latching and breastfeeding as soon as you and Baby are ready.

If you are feeling really engorged (that is, your breasts are over-full) when your fuller milk comes in, you can also pump for a few minutes to relieve engorgement. For more on pumping, see page 69.

A Word on Nipple Confusion

It is recommended that parents hold off on bottles and pacifiers until breastfeeding is well established so that babies can focus on mastering one skill before trying another. For the baby, extracting milk from Mom's breast requires a different technique that can sometimes be more difficult than removing milk from a bottle. However, there are some instances when a pacifier or bottle might be introduced to a newborn. Babies in the NICU are given pacifiers to help soothe them when they are separated from their parents. In some hospitals, even breastfeeding babies might be given a bottle at night so Mom can get rest. Ask your hospital representative what its policy is, and insist on being awakened if you don't want your baby bottle-fed. Also, babies who are not latching or are struggling to latch are given bottles, as Rule #1 is "Feed the baby." Sometimes this can cause nipple confusion, because a pacifier and bottle nipple feel different than a bare breast. This may also cause flow preference, when a baby prefers the easy flow of the bottle to the breast. However, if your circumstance necessitates a pacifier or bottle early on, it doesn't mean that breastfeeding will not work. It just means you might need some extra assistance getting over these temporary hurdles when your baby is ready.

Breastfeeding at Home

Once you are back at home in your own space, without constant interruptions by medical professionals, you will want to find your own breastfeeding rhythm and setup. Try out different locations in your home to see which is most comfortable. Consider your couch, a rocking chair or glider, and your bed. Make a breastfeeding basket that has all of the supplies you need before, during, and after your breastfeeding session (see basket ideas in Top Breastfeeding Tips, page 48). As mentioned, babies need to feed eight or more

TONGUE TIES

A tongue tie is a band of tissue that connects the under-side of the tongue to the floor of the mouth. If this band is tight, it can restrict Baby's tongue movement, making it difficult to breastfeed or even bottle-feed. Some babies can breastfeed with a tongue tie if the band is flexible and doesn't limit the tongue's mobility to create a seal and provide suction while breastfeeding. If your baby's tongue cannot move appropriately while breast-feeding, you might see the following signs:

- Baby stops gaining weight well (less than 5 to 8 ounces per week for the first four months)
- Baby is compressing Mom's nipples and causing pain
- Baby seems excessively gassy and has reflux symptoms
- Baby cannot maintain a good seal on the breast and/or bottle
- Baby is unable to latch without the nipple shield
- Mom's milk supply goes down
- Mom has recurrent plugged ducts and/or milk blisters
- Baby is having a difficult time with solids

If your baby's tongue tie appears to be causing any of these symptoms, have your baby assessed by an IBCLC to confirm. He or she might recommend having your baby's tongue tie released. This quick-release procedure, called a frenectomy, can be performed by an ear, nose, and throat specialist; a pediatric dentist; and some pediatricians and IBCLCs.

times in 24 hours, which is about every two or three hours. Until your baby is back to his birth weight (ideally by two weeks of age), you may need to wake him to feed if he is still sleeping three hours after you last started breastfeeding. This will ensure that you get in at least eight feedings in 24 hours. Babies typically feed for about 20 to 40 minutes, with time spent on both breasts during each feeding session. Many moms find it helpful to start on the same breast that they ended with at the last breastfeeding session.

Top Breastfeeding Tips

Not all breastfeeding tips are specifically about latching and positioning. Here are some additional recommendations to make breastfeeding as easy as possible:

Download a breastfeeding app. For the first few weeks, you'll want to keep track of how often your baby breastfeeds and how many pees and poops she has. An app helps keep track so you don't have to try to remember.

Create a breastfeeding basket. Whether you breastfeed in your room, living room, nursery, or other space, you can bring this basket of stuff along with you so you have everything you need while breastfeeding. Include diapers, wipes, extra baby clothing, burp cloth, water bottle (it's thirsty work!), nipple cream, breast pads, lip balm (such as ChapStick), phone charger, hair tie, and so on.

Have someone set up a meal train for your family. To produce milk, you need a steady amount of calories—over 2,000 per day. If friends bring food, they get to meet your baby, too! Plus, it's one fewer thing you have to think about after your baby arrives.

If you are struggling, get help ASAP! Don't wait until you are ready to quit before calling in reinforcements. Go to a support group. Call a lactation consultant.

Don't quit on your hardest day. Mastering breastfeeding can take several weeks to several months, depending on the situation. It is a new skill for both you and your baby. One terrible feeding or day of feedings doesn't mean tomorrow will look the same way. Reach out for help and support before throwing in the towel. You'll be glad you did!

Your Milk Supply

Your milk supply will drastically increase over the first two weeks after your baby's birth. As you will recall, your colostrum should transition to a fuller milk by Day 3 to 5. This breakdown shows approximately how much your baby should be taking in per feeding, based on age:

DAY 1	5 to 7 ml (1 teaspoon) colostrum
DAY 3	25 to 30 ml (1 ounce) transitional breastmilk
DAY 7	45 ml (1½ ounces) breastmilk
DAY 10	60 ml (2 ounces) breastmilk
DAY 14	75 to 90 ml (2½ to 3 ounces) breastmilk

Most women feel like their breasts get heavier and tighter when their fuller milk comes in. This is a great sign—you want your breasts to get heavier with milk! Some moms, especially moms who have breastfed before, find that their milk supply comes in more quickly and robustly than with their previous child. Frequent feedings and milk removal will help keep this fullness at a manageable level so you don't become terribly uncomfortable.

HOW WILL I KNOW IF BABY IS GETTING ENOUGH?

- Baby is peeing and pooping regularly (minimum of once each on Day 1, twice each on Day 2, continuing to at least five times each by Day 5 and beyond)
- Baby stops losing weight by Day 3 and begins to gain 1 ounce per day
- Baby is back to birth weight by Day 14
- Baby seems satisfied and content after breastfeeding and can usually go one or two hours before wanting to feed again

WHAT ARE SIGNS THAT BABY IS NOT GETTING ENOUGH?

- Baby loses more than 10 percent of his birth weight
- Baby is not gaining weight even after your fuller milk comes in
- Baby is not peeing and pooping often enough (see previous list)
- Baby seems lethargic and too sleepy to eat well
- Baby is excessively fussy and doesn't seem content after feeding

These are all good reasons to seek breastfeeding support and assistance.

> JUST THE FACTS
>
> Breastfeeding allows your body to recover from pregnancy and childbirth more quickly. The hormones released when you breastfeed make your uterus contract back to its pre-pregnancy size.
>
> —OFFICE ON WOMEN'S HEALTH,
> US DEPARTMENT OF HEALTH AND HUMAN SERVICES

Dealing with Discomfort and Pain

Beware of the Internet—it's full of horror stories about how painful breastfeeding is. These stories could scare even the most determined breastfeeder. The truth is, breastfeeding is generally comfortable and enjoyable, and nipple and breast pain while breastfeeding is *not* normal.

Sore or Cracked Nipples

For the first few weeks, some nipple tenderness is normal. This is a lot of stimulation for one part of your body. Oftentimes, this tenderness is present just with Baby's initial latch and then subsides within the first minute or so of suckling. Nipple tenderness should subside altogether within the first two weeks of breastfeeding, as your milk increases and becomes easier for your baby to get out.

For women who experience significant nipple pain, this is your body's way of telling you that something needs to be fixed. Significant nipple pain and cracked nipples can happen for a variety of reasons: shallow latch, tongue tie, chompy suck, and difficulties with positioning Baby. So, go back to basics: Aim your nipple for your baby's nose. Hug your baby into your torso to provide maximum support. Make sure your baby has a wide latch. After breastfeeding, lubricate your nipples with a nipple cream or expressed breastmilk to keep them from getting too dry in between feedings.

As you work to figure out what is causing your sore or cracked nipples, here are some remedies to get you through the discomfort and put you back on track for comfortable breastfeeding.

Nipple cream   Expressed breastmilk can lubricate your nipples after a feeding, but there are also many creams, gels, and oils that can help keep your nipples moist in between feedings and help heal cracked nipples. Check out organic nipple balms, lanolin, and coconut oil. All-purpose nipple ointment (see page 137) and MEDIHONEY paste are great for healing really cracked nipples.

Gel pads   Made by several different companies, these gel pads are designed for wet wound management. They keep your nipples moist in between feedings to allow for maximum healing when cracked.

Nipple shield   This is a thin piece of silicone that goes over your nipple, helping Baby latch on when having difficulties. It also creates a barrier over your nipple to allow for healing when cracked. Nipple shields should always be used under the guidance of a lactation consultant, for although they can be very helpful, they can also sometimes create challenges, such as difficulties removing milk effectively and lowering Mom's milk supply. They are meant for temporary use.

If the pain doesn't subside or gets worse, contact a lactation consultant to save your nipples as soon as possible!

Engorgement

Typically, engorgement happens between Days 3 and 7—this is when your breasts get too full with milk, sometimes making it difficult for your baby or even the pump to remove. However, there are some very easy ways to prevent and treat uncomfortable engorgement. To prevent engorgement, put your baby to the breast often (eight or more times in 24 hours), as frequent emptying of your breasts keeps fullness to a manageable level. A deep, wide latch will also ensure that your baby is able to remove milk effectively each time she breastfeeds. If your breasts are feeling uncomfortable and overly full despite frequent breastfeeding, there are several things you can do:

- To reduce swelling, use cold compresses in between feedings. Try a bag of frozen peas, or consider buying a sack of seeds or rice, which you can put in the freezer so it's very cold before you place it on your breasts. See Resources (page 134) for recommendations.
- To relieve engorgement and help milk come out more easily, use warmth. Some of the simplest ways are to take a warm shower or place a warm washcloth on your breasts right before feedings. Relaxing and gently massaging your breasts in a warm shower can even stimulate spontaneous milk letdown. If you have a sack of seeds or rice, it works not only for cooling but for warmth, too. Just warm it up in the microwave before placing on your breasts.
- If your breasts are too tight to latch your baby, try a techinque called reverse pressure softening to disperse fluid and soften your areola so that your baby can latch more easily. You can also try therapeutic breast massage (see Resources, page 134) to relieve tight areas in your breasts.
- If your breasts are still really full after breastfeeding, you can hand express (see Resources, page 134) or pump for just a few minutes to see if that relieves some of the excess pressure.
- Note that unresolved engorgement can lead to plugged ducts, as well. To treat plugged ducts, see page 76.

EATING TO SUPPORT BREASTFEEDING

It is important to be well nourished in order to produce breastmilk and heal from delivery. Expect your appetite to be high and don't be afraid to honor it. Breastfeeding requires approximately 500 extra calories a day, so it is recommended to eat at least 2,000 calories per day. Amid the chaos of a newborn, visitors, and healing from delivery, it's very easy to forget to eat or to feel unprepared or unable to get adequate meals when you need them. Try these tips for easing the nutrition transition:

- Ask your partner, family members, and friends to take over grocery shopping, planning, and meal prep for at least the first few weeks or months after having your baby, if at all possible.

- Have someone coordinate a meal train.

- Make extra food at dinnertime so you can eat the leftovers for breakfast and lunch.

- Become best friends with your Crock-Pot or Instant Pot.

- Use shop-from-home services, if your grocery store offers them, so you can stock up on convenient and healthy options without having to leave the house.

Here are a few recommendations for snacks and meals just to get you started. Check the Resources section (page 134) for some recipe website and book recommendations.

BREAKFAST

- Eggs
- Granola with milk or Greek yogurt
- Leftovers
- Overnight oats with nuts and fruit
- Power smoothies made from fresh or frozen fruit, coconut water, chia seeds, protein powder, and greens
- Avocado toast

LUNCH/DINNER

- Stews/soups (super easy to make in a Crock-Pot)
- High-quality proteins like wild-caught fish, beef, chicken, or pork
- Leafy greens and vegetables
- Beans and legumes
- Vegetable quiche

SNACKS

- Guacamole
- Hummus
- Veggie sticks
- Tuna and chicken salad
- Jerky
- Hardboiled eggs
- Seaweed
- Leftovers
- Cheese
- Trail mix of nuts, seeds, and dried fruits

Caring for Yourself

Becoming a new mom can feel very overwhelming. This is a time of colossal change. I remember sitting on my bed, five days post-partum, sobbing my eyes out while laughing at the same time. My husband came into our room and was concerned that I was having some sort of psychotic episode. I immediately reassured him that I was okay but just felt very overcome by emotions. I was so in love with our baby boy, who was sleeping soundly next to me, but also overwhelmed about breastfeeding, parenting, and life in general. Plus, my crotch was killing me post-"surprise" episiotomy. So, I was crying to relieve all that emotion and discomfort but now laughing because I had been crying for about 10 minutes and it seemed weirdly funny to me. So, yes, it is completely normal to feel all over the place, emotionally. Your hormones are dipping and spiking. You may be recovering from physical and/or emotional pain. It's a lot to carry!

Whenever you find yourself feeling overcome by emotions, remember to take everything day by day, feeding by feeding. Connect with friends who have been through this before, who can offer encouragement and support. Ask for help—you are not in this alone. Get as much rest as possible, as sleep deprivation can make things seem much more overwhelming. Snuggle with your sleeping baby, as her breath, her scent, and her body have magical calming properties.

Frequently Asked Questions

IF I DON'T FEEL A LETDOWN, IS MY BABY NOT GETTING MILK?

Letdown is your milk releasing from your milk ducts. Most women experience several letdowns per breastfeeding session, but not all mothers feel their letdowns. If your baby has several periods of swallowing every one to three sucks, then your baby is getting milk during your letdown.

HOW WILL I KNOW IF I NEED TO USE FORMULA?

If your baby has lost more than 10 percent of his birth weight or isn't gaining about 1 ounce a day by Days 3 to 5, supplementation might be recommended. The first recommended option for supplementation is Mom's pumped milk, if you are able to pump or hand express. The second option would be donor milk, from either a milk bank or informal milk sharing. The third option would be formula. Any type of supplementation should be temporary as you work through your breastfeeding challenges.

IF MY MILK IS DELAYED COMING IN, WILL I BE ABLE TO EVER MEET MY BABY'S NEED?

That is the hope. Cesarean birth, significant swelling or edema, high blood pressure, gestational diabetes, significant blood loss, and other issues can sometimes delay Mom's fuller milk coming in. If you've had these issues, you will want to meet with a lactation consultant right after birth and possibly start pumping a bit in addition to breastfeeding. This extra breast stimulation can help bring in your milk supply more quickly.

I HAVE FLAT NIPPLES. WILL THIS MAKE IT MORE DIFFICULT FOR MY BABY TO BREASTFEED?

It shouldn't. Keep in mind that babies "breastfeed," not "nipple feed." As long as your baby gets enough breast tissue into his mouth when latching, it really shouldn't matter whether you have flat or everted nipples. Some babies with high palates or tongue ties can have more difficulty latching onto flat nipples. Try to make a "breast sandwich" (see page 32) to bring more of your areola into Baby's mouth, which can definitely help with latching.

While breastfeeding is a natural
act, it is also a learned behaviour.
An extensive body of research has
demonstrated that mothers and other
caregivers require active support for
establishing and sustaining appropriate
breastfeeding practices.

—WORLD HEALTH ORGANIZATION

Two Weeks to Three Months

. . . .

Okay, first two weeks down—awesome job, mama! At this point, some moms feel like they are getting the hang of breastfeeding. Confidence is building as they see their babies gaining weight and as latching gets easier. Other moms might still feel like they are struggling with breastfeeding, second-guessing themselves and perhaps questioning their commitment to breastfeeding.

If you are in the first camp, your thoughts will move toward making breastfeeding even more comfortable, keeping Baby awake during feedings, not having to wake Baby in the middle of the night to feed, breastfeeding in public, considering when to start pumping and storing milk for future bottles, and so on.

If you are in the second camp, you may start to feel disappointed and concerned that breastfeeding may not get easier. Please continue to pursue support while keeping this important thought in mind: You and your baby are learning a new skill, which can sometimes take six to 12 weeks to really establish, while hopefully improving along the way. Most moms find that their com-mitment truly pays off, if they can harness the necessary support and just hang in there. Meanwhile, don't compare your situation to others. Sometimes it just takes certain babies and moms a bit more time to get their groove, making success that much sweeter.

When Breastfeeding Is Going Well

With each passing week, you should notice that breastfeeding con-tinues to get easier and more enjoyable. Eventually you'll be able to read your baby's signs to know when she is full. She'll stay awake more easily while breastfeeding. She will also become more effi-cient, so those 20- to 40-minute breastfeeding sessions will shorten. Comfortable latching will become more consistent. Daytime feed-ings will still continue every two to three hours, but Baby might start to sleep a bit longer between feedings at night. Nipple soreness should be a thing of the past! Breastfeeding in public won't seem so overwhelming, as your baby will take minimal time to latch.

When Breastfeeding Is a Struggle

When breastfeeding isn't going smoothly, it can seem incredibly overwhelming and disappointing, especially when compounded by a lack of sleep and fluctuating hormones. Look for online or in-person support to get encouragement and advice. Finding a sup-portive IBCLC can help relieve anxiety and stress, as this person is trained to offer personalized advice, guidance, and emotional support as you work toward your personal breastfeeding goals. Here are some common struggles, and suggestions for working through them:

Trouble latching Try different breastfeeding positions to see if one works better than the others. Have your baby assessed for a tongue tie. Ask your pediatrician or IBCLC about bodywork/relaxation methods such as craniosacral therapy (see page 130), chiropractic care, and occupational therapy to help improve your baby's latch and tongue suction.

Slow weight gain Find a support group (or work with a lactation consultant) where you can weigh your baby before and after a breastfeeding session to see how much he is taking in and how much more he needs to get his weight back on track.

Low milk supply Have your baby's feeding session and your breasts assessed by an IBCLC to see what additional strategies can help increase your milk supply. Find ways to supplement that are most supportive of breastfeeding (like supplementing at the breast) and will help alleviate the need to supplement as soon as possible.

Fussy or gassy baby Talk with your pediatrician or IBCLC about the possibility of reflux or food intolerances and some remedies.

Depressed or anxious feelings If you are feeling more depressed or anxious than what you feel should be normal for this postpartum time period, seek assistance from your health care provider or a therapist. Online resources, such as postpartum.net, can also provide information and guidance.

Remember, you are not in this alone. There are excellent resources and practical solutions to nearly any challenge you may face. I encourage you to advocate for the needs of you and your baby and to find the right team of individuals to support you.

> JUST THE FACTS
> A mother's perception of her partner's attitude toward breastfeeding is one of the greatest factors influencing her decision to breastfeed.
> —HEALTHYCHILDREN.ORG

Increasing Milk Production

The topic of milk supply is a massive one, as many breastfeeding moms wonder whether they are making enough milk for their babies. Milk supply is based on several components: supply and demand, postpartum hormones, and breast tissue. The more your baby or pump "requests" milk, the more your body will make.

As mentioned, your milk supply starts low in quantity and continues to increase daily over the first two weeks, spurred by frequent feedings. You will also experience a huge spike in the hormone prolactin, which speeds up milk production. Glandular tissue inside the breast also continues to grow after your baby is born.

FACING THE SCALE

One thing they forget to tell you is that after you have a baby, you still look like you are four to six months pregnant for at least a few weeks to a few months after birth! And although breastfeeding burns plenty of calories, many women find that their bodies still hold on to a few extra pounds while breastfeeding, in order to continue to make a robust milk supply. When you're feeling ready, incorporating some self-care and exercise can be profoundly beneficial for your health, energy level, and emotional well-being. Joining a mommy-and-me yoga class or exercise group can foster vital connections with other new moms while negating the need for childcare. Try not to stress over the scale. Over time, your body will morph into shape, sometimes with a few extra curves, which is not a bad thing!

Mom has a higher risk for low milk supply when:

- Baby is not effectively breastfeeding or feeding frequently enough.
- she has a history of hormonal imbalances such as thyroid condition, polycystic ovary syndrome, or fertility challenges.
- she had postpartum hemorrhage or retained placenta.
- she has a history of hypoplasia or breast surgery.

The following recommendations can be helpful for boosting your milk supply. However, if you begin to see signs that your milk supply needs a boost, contact an IBCLC as soon as possible to assess why this is happening. These recommendations are most effective only when any cause of low milk supply is identified and addressed.

To increase milk supply, use these techniques:

Increase breastfeeding frequency. If your baby is an effective nurser, add in a few additional breastfeeding sessions each day.

Pump after breastfeeding. Pumping with a double electric pump for 15 minutes after breastfeeding provides additional stimulation and can pull out a bit of leftover milk, especially when Baby isn't breastfeeding well.

Supplement Baby at breast. An at-breast supplementation system (see Resources, page 134) can provide Baby with supplemented pumped milk, donor milk, or formula while she breastfeeds. Feeding Baby this way can also help her stay actively sucking while breastfeeding, providing Mom with helpful stimulation.

Consider an herbal galactagogue. The most common herbal recommendations are fenugreek (not recommended if you have a thyroid condition or diabetes), moringa, blessed thistle, alfalfa, goat's rue (builds glandular tissue), and shatavari (balances hormones).

Eat lactogenic foods. Oats, millet, barley, leafy green vegetables, almonds, cashews, brewer's yeast, fennel, beets, and iron-rich vegetables and meats are a few foods that can boost milk supply. See Resources (page 134) for additional information.

Try acupuncture. This practice increases blood flow, and milk is made from blood.

Have your hormone levels tested. Make sure they are within normal range.

Inquire about prescription medication. Reglan (increases prolactin), domperidone (increases prolactin), and metformin (stabilizes blood sugar) can help, under the guidance of a medical professional.

Ensuring Good Nutrition for You and Baby

Even after your baby is born, you'll still be eating for two. Breast-feeding mothers need to eat at least 2,000 calories per day to ensure a robust milk supply. After delivery, it is important to replenish Mom's iron stores. Good iron sources include lean ground beef, liver, turkey legs, tuna, eggs, shrimp, beans, lentils, tofu, molasses, spinach, peanut butter, and brown rice.

It's important to keep taking a high-quality prenatal vitamin and fish oil to ensure that you produce milk that is full of the vitamins, minerals, and essential fatty acids Baby needs for growth and development. Other foods that have notable health benefits include fish rich in omega-3s for Baby's brain development, iodine-rich seaweed for Baby's brain and metabolism, and healthy proteins and fats. Vitamin D_3 and calcium help build strong bones, cell membranes, hormones, and more.

There are a few foods that might affect your baby's mood in a negative way. Some babies react poorly to caffeine, especially if you had cut out caffeinated drinks while pregnant. Caffeine can make Baby more irritable or fussy, or cause difficulty sleeping. Fortunately, this sensitivity often passes as Baby gets older. Some babies also react when Mom consumes alcohol. Alcohol can temporarily decrease the milk supply and inhibit letdown, which can frustrate Baby while breastfeeding.

Some babies react to foods that Mom is eating, as they can cause excessive gas, fussiness, and mucus in Baby's poops. This occurs when Mom's body does not break down foods effectively, causing her digestive system to leak undigested proteins into her bloodstream, which then move into her breastmilk. If you have food intolerances, try to avoid these foods while breastfeeding so your baby doesn't have a reaction to them. An IBCLC or nutritionist can help identify the foods that are causing a reaction so you can remove them from your diet.

JUST THE FACTS
Human milk is the only single food that meets all the nutritional requirements to sustain life.
—COUNSELING THE NURSING MOTHER

SURVIVING THE
WITCHING HOUR

Most babies have a certain time of day or night when they seem insatiable or demanding. Your baby might feed every hour for a few hours, seemingly satisfied after a feeding, and then wake up crying for more just 30 minutes later. This is also commonly called the witching hour. For the first few weeks, babies tend to be more awake and want to cluster feed—that is, feed frequently in bursts—in the middle of the night. After the first few weeks, most babies settle back in more easily after nighttime feedings and move their witching hour(s) to right around dinnertime.

Babies cluster feed for several reasons. One, they are trying to unwind after feeling overstimulated by their day. There is nothing more calming than latching on and falling asleep on Mom. Two, by the late afternoon or early evening, many moms feel their milk supply is not as robust as it was in the morning. So babies will need to feed more frequently at this time. Babies will also cluster feed during growth spurts (see page 68) as well as when they don't feel well, are teething, and are going through a developmental milestone.

To survive these cluster-feeding sessions:

- wear your baby in a carrier, sling, or wrap. You can breastfeed in these, and keep Baby calm and close while he sleeps between feeding sessions.
- get a break by taking your baby on a walk.
- ask for help so you can get a mini break.
- make dinner early, then heat it up when hungry.
- keep in mind that this is temporary and usually subsides around three months.

Demand Feeding versus Scheduled Feedings

Two of the most common questions moms ask are *When are feedings going to become more predictable?* and *When can I start to put my baby on a schedule?*

For the first few weeks, you are encouraged to wake your baby if three hours have passed since he last fed. However, once he is back to birth weight, on-demand feeding is usually the recommended way to feed your baby in the early days, weeks, and months.

Demand Feeding

Feeding your baby "on demand" simply means not worrying about the clock. You feed your baby whenever he shows you he is hungry. Common ways your baby will show you this include licking his lips, sticking out his tongue, rooting around, sucking on his hands, and so on. Feeding your baby on demand also means that you don't "time" the feedings (such as 15 minutes per side), but rather, you allow him to feed until he is satisfied. It can be confusing to know when your baby's had enough, but some good cues are when he unlatches himself from the breast and doesn't try to get back on and when he falls asleep at the breast and feels very relaxed and loose when you lift his arm.

There are many benefits to on-demand feeding. In the immediate days following birth, putting your baby to your breast in response to any and all hunger cues is excellent for bringing in a full milk supply. As he gets older, on-demand feeding helps ensure that he gets enough milk to grow properly. Mothers have different storage capacities in their breasts, and all babies take in different amounts; even the same baby will take differing amounts throughout the day.

Scheduled Feeding

Scheduled feeding is when a parent chooses a timed feeding interval based on things like the baby's weight or age, and feeds her only at these intervals, regardless of her cues or readiness. One thing to keep in mind is that your baby is likely to start to shape her own feeding behavior into a more predictable schedule by six to 12 weeks of age. Trying to make/force/help her do that before she is ready only makes for a stressed-out mama and a cranky baby, if she is not developmentally ready for this.

Some mothers might feel overworked and tired from being available all of the time to breastfeed on demand. This is a common stress for many moms in the early weeks, but be encouraged: it passes. It might seem like your baby is feeding ALL. THE. TIME. in those first six weeks or so, but as time goes on, your baby will begin to form his own schedule—or at least you'll grow better accustomed to his pattern and behaviors. A great solution to feeling overwhelmed is to breastfeed in a carrier, which allows you to not be chained to the couch when Baby is hungry. For the overtired mom, it's okay to bring your baby into bed at night. (See page 81 for safe bedsharing guidelines.) Don't let anyone else dictate what's right or wrong here; you're the one taking the night shift! This often helps everyone get more rest. Last, if you are feeling overwhelmed, you can also incorporate a bit of pumping and bottle-feeding so others can help feed Baby when you need a break.

Growth Spurts

Just when you think things are starting to fall into place, your baby will experience a growth spurt and throw things out of whack for a few days! All babies go through growth spurts, usually around two weeks, four weeks, six weeks, three months, and six months. These are also the times when a mom will go through a hormonal change, with the potential to decrease her milk supply. So yes, Mother Nature has paired you with a voracious being that seemingly wants to eat nonstop for about three days. The good news is that extra breast stimulation will help balance and boost your milk supply against those crazy hormones.

The silver lining to this nonstop feeding frenzy? As soon as it's over, your baby will likely spend the next day taking very long naps to recover from this eating marathon, giving you some time to rest and recuperate. If Baby doesn't seem satisfied after eating and is feeding constantly for more than a few days, check in with a breastfeeding support group or your pediatrician to make sure that your baby is gaining weight well and feeding effectively.

Pumping Breastmilk

Pumps come in many shapes, sizes, and styles, and with various bells and whistles. If you haven't yet, take out all of the pieces, read the manual, and sterilize anything that needs to be cleaned before the first use. If you didn't use your pump in the first few weeks, pull it out about three to six weeks postpartum. That is the perfect time to introduce a bottle to your baby, and if using breastmilk, you will need to pump to get it. For moms who plan to return to work, pumping once a day, maybe after a morning breastfeeding session, will help get some of that precious liquid gold in your freezer.

Here are different types of pumps you can choose from:

Manual Pumps

Manual pumps do not have batteries. The suction and speed depend on how fast or slow you squeeze your hand. These can be fantastic for occasional use such as after a feeding session, while on vacation, or for collecting milk for an occasional bottle. However, these pumps will rarely keep up a milk supply for moms pumping a few times a day.

Electric Pumps (Single-Person Use)

These pumps come as single or double pumps and either plug in or run on batteries. Pumping both breasts at the same time can maximize efficiency. These pumps usually have a suction dial (to adjust the suction) and a speed dial (to adjust pump speed). Most manuals have a recommended way to use these dials, but you'll find what works best for you. These pumps are effective for maintaining your milk supply once it is fully in.

Electric Pumps (Multiple Users)

These are double electric pumps, also called hospital-grade pumps. They are the flagship of the pump industry. Their motors are the most consistent and are meant to last longer than their non-hospital-grade counterparts. Some are available for purchase, while others can be rented from a hospital or lactation consultant. These pumps are often recommended to bring in or increase a milk supply or for use by moms who are exclusively pumping.

Flanges

The flange is the funnel-shaped piece of equipment that suctions to your breast during pumping and draws milk from your nipple. The correct flange size is so important for making your pump work for you—just like Goldilocks and the Three Bears! Flanges that are too small Ⓐ can cause significant pain in your nipples and areolas as they rub up against the side of the plastic. Flanges that are too large won't remove milk well, which can be uncomfortable and frustrating. In illustration Ⓑ, the the flange is too big relative to the breast and so the breast does not rest firmly against the flange. In illustration Ⓒ the flange is so large that there is a sliver of space between the flange and the breast that prevents the suction from taking hold. Flanges that are just the right size Ⓓ should remove your milk in a reasonable amount of time (about 15 minutes), feel comfortable (no chafing), and be easy to use. About ½ inch of your areola should

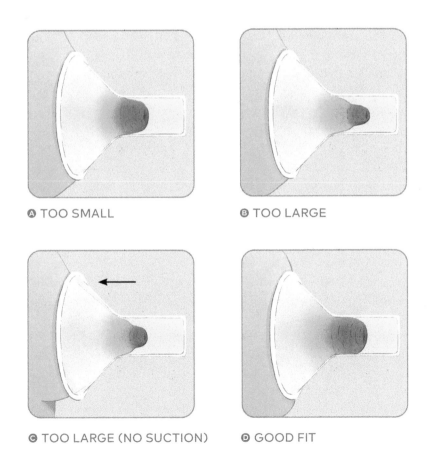

Ⓐ TOO SMALL

Ⓑ TOO LARGE

Ⓒ TOO LARGE (NO SUCTION)

Ⓓ GOOD FIT

go into the tunnel of the flange, with space completely around your entire nipple, throughout the pumping session.

It is not recommended to share a pump unless it is meant for multiple users, like a hospital-grade pump. If you end up getting a pump from a friend or family member, make sure to replace all of the flange pieces and tubing, and have the suction checked to make sure it is functioning at maximum capacity.

Storing Breastmilk

If you don't immediately offer your pumped milk to your baby, you will need to store it in either the refrigerator or freezer. A chart on page 129 lists the specific guidelines for safe milk storage. If your baby doesn't finish all of the pumped milk in the bottle, you can place it back into the refrigerator to be used within the next few hours. Don't combine milk from different pumping sessions for storage unless they are already the same temperature.

Options abound for storing pumped milk. Breastmilk freezer bags store up to 5 or 6 ounces of pumped milk. Some families prefer to store milk in bottles or mason jars. When doing this, leave some space at the top of the container so the container doesn't burst during the freezing process. There are also specially made frozen milk trays that look like ice cube trays with a lid. Plan to store your frozen milk in 2- to 4-ounce increments, since your baby's appetite will change over time. Also, label each bag or container with the date you froze the milk and the quantity. Cycle through your frozen milk, using the oldest milk first, so it doesn't have a chance to go bad.

BREASTFEEDING AND ALCOHOL

Current research says that occasional use of alcohol (one to two drinks over the course of a few hours) does not appear to be harmful to the nursing baby. The American Academy of Pediatrics Section on Breastfeeding states, "Ingestion of alcoholic beverages should be minimized and limited to an occasional intake but no more than 0.5 grams alcohol per kg body weight, which for a 60 kg (132-pound) mother is approximately 2 ounces of liquor, 8 ounces of wine, or 2 beers. Nursing should take place 2 hours or longer after the alcohol intake to minimize its concentration in the ingested milk."

In general, if you are sober enough to drive, you are considered by current studies sober enough to breast-feed. Less than 2 percent of the alcohol consumed by the mother reaches her blood and milk. Alcohol peaks in Mom's blood and milk approximately half an hour to one hour after drinking (with considerable variation depending upon how much food was eaten in the same time period, Mom's body weight and percentage of body fat, etc.). Alcohol does not accumulate in breastmilk, but leaves the milk as it leaves the blood, so when your blood alcohol levels are back down, so are your milk alcohol levels. There is no need to "pump and dump," unless your breasts feel very uncomfortable and full.

Breastfeeding in Public

My personal opinion lines up nicely with how author David Allen put it: "Anybody offended by breastfeeding is staring too hard." Even though breastfeeding in public continues to be a very controversial topic, you can make it work for you and everyone around you. Breastfeeding your baby on the go allows you to get out of the house and get back into the activities that you enjoyed before your baby arrived. If you are nervous about breastfeeding in public, practice at home first in front of a mirror, so you can see how little of your breast is actually exposed while breastfeeding. Pick up some nursing-friendly shirts and tanks so you don't have to remove any clothing while feeding. Some moms prefer to breastfeed with a nursing cover, while others don't use a cover at all. Some moms even master breastfeeding in a carrier, wrap, or sling. Find what makes you most comfortable and go for it!

It is uncommon for others to make a negative comment about nursing in public, as it so often goes unnoticed. If you are concerned that someone might say something negative about your breastfeeding in public, read up on your state law and feel free to educate anyone who needs it. Memorize a reply you can share if someone approaches you, such as "Thank you for being concerned for my baby. He'd appreciate it if you would give him some space so he can continue to eat." Remind those around you that breastfeeding is important for you and your baby's health and well-being and that if they are uncomfortable, they are welcome to move somewhere away from you, like to another state!

A Mom's Story
ANNALIESE

I've never been one to nurse in public without a cover, especially after reading all of the stories online about people getting yelled at, stared at, or just overall treated rudely. My family went out with a friend and her daughter to a local park, where the kids were playing on a large climbing sculpture. My son started crying, and my spouse decided that our baby was hungry. I had thought we'd be able to get through this trip without needing to breastfeed, and we had forgotten to bring a blanket with us. So I took my son and sat on one of the cement benches under the overhang and kind of curled into the corner. My eight-year-old wanted me to watch him, so I turned toward him after I got the baby latched. At one point a female and a male were walking by, and after they were about 10 steps past me, the female turned around and yelled, "I just wanted to let you know, you rock!" I laughed because I didn't really do anything except breastfeed in public, but it made me feel better about my decision.

Common Problems and Solutions

A few common challenges can arise while breastfeeding. Here's how to prevent and treat them:

Cracked nipples Cracked nipples can be caused by a baby not latching correctly or having a tongue tie. To prevent cracked nipples, focus on getting the widest latch possible, making sure your baby's lips are flanged (like fish lips). Your nipples should be nice and round when your baby unlatches—not pinched, creased, or beveled like a lipstick. Read more in Solutions for Sore or Cracked Nipples and Engorgement (page 51).

Plugged ducts Plugged ducts are caused when your milk ducts get backed up, causing inflammation. They feel like a hard knot in your breast. Sometimes they are really small, and other times a large section of your breast can feel very tight and sore. Frequent feedings and good milk removal will help prevent plugged ducts. If you get a plugged duct, use cold compresses and ibuprofen between feedings to reduce inflammation, and utilize warm compresses or a hot shower right before feeding to help release your milk more easily. Therapeutic breast massage (see Resources, page 134) and gentle massage with the back of an electric toothbrush can also help move the milk along.

Thrush Thrush is a yeast infection that can affect Mom and Baby. Mom's nipples might look raw and red, and they may itch or burn while feeding and in between feedings. Baby might have a thick white coating on her tongue and cheeks and/or a bad diaper rash. Thrush can be caused by cracked nipples, an overgrowth in yeast in Mom or Baby, or when either Mom or Baby takes antibiotics. You can prevent thrush by healing your nipples as quickly as possible and taking a quality, refrigerated probiotic to colonize your gut with good bacteria. You might ask your IBCLC, ob-gyn, midwife, or pediatrician about over-the-counter, topical, oral, or prescription medications to clear up the infection.

Mastitis Mastitis is an infection in the milk duct, usually caused by an unresolved plugged duct or cracked nipple. Moms are most prone to mastitis in the first few weeks, when the body's immune system is at its lowest, and when Baby or pump is not effectively removing milk. Common symptoms include red streaks on the breast, very tender breasts, a fever of over 102°F, and feeling like you have the flu. Mastitis can be prevented by ensuring frequent, regular feedings; removing milk by pump if Baby is having a difficult time breastfeeding; healing cracked nipples as soon as possible; and getting as much rest as possible during those first few weeks postpartum. Mastitis can often be treated when caught early, with cold or castor-oil compresses on the swollen area, warm showers or compresses before feeding, therapeutic breast massage, immunity-boosting herbs (like echinacea, zinc, and vitamin C), and anti-inflammatories (like ibuprofen and turmeric). Sometimes antibiotics are necessary to heal the infection.

Milk blister A milk blister (also known as a bleb) is a white spot at the tip of your nipple that looks like a pimple and hurts like heck. Milk blisters can be caused by thick milk being released by a plugged duct or from Baby compressing your nipple while feeding. Essentially, one of the openings in your nipple has gotten clogged and needs to be released. If your baby is constantly creating a ridge on your nipple while feeding, you'll want to resolve this issue to lower your future risk of milk blisters. Milk blisters can be treated by placing a cotton ball soaked with coconut oil on your nipple (in your bra) in between feedings or by soaking your breast in a bowl of very warm water mixed with Epsom salts a few times a day.

Getting a Breastfed Baby
to Take a Bottle

A good window of opportunity to offer your baby his first bottle is between three and six weeks of age. At this time, your baby will still have his innate sucking reflex, which stimulates him to suck when the roof of his mouth is stroked. By 10 to 12 weeks, this sucking reflex diminishes, making it more difficult to introduce a bottle after this time. Many mothers worry about nipple confusion; however, that is fairly uncommon if breastfeeding is going well.

When offering a bottle to your breastfed baby, use the paced bottle-feeding method. This method will help your baby take in less air and bottle-feed comfortably as well as slow down the flow so Baby has to work to get the milk out. Here's how:

1. Hold your baby in a semireclined position.

2. Tickle his lips with the bottle nipple, and insert the bottle once he opens his mouth. Make sure his lips are flanged, just like on the breast.

3. Hold the bottle horizontally and burp your baby after every ounce, and again at the end of the feeding.

If your baby doesn't take the bottle on the first attempt, consider trying a different bottle with a different nipple shape. Change the temperature of the pumped milk. Hold your baby in a different position. And if your baby downright refuses the bottle, meet with a lactation consultant, who can assess the cause for bottle rejection and offer additional suggestions.

Baby Sleep and Breastfeeding

Is your baby sleeping through the night?

This will probably be the most annoying question you receive as a new parent, especially if the answer is no. Our society's expectations of how many consecutive hours an infant should sleep are, unfortunately, completely unrealistic. So, as a sleep-deprived parent confronted with this ubiquitous question, you may suddenly feel like you are doing everything wrong with your baby if she is not sleeping through the night at six weeks. You might even start Googling tips for "sleep training," but this practice is definitely not recommended for an infant, as it can cause your baby to stop gaining weight well and sabotage your milk supply. Instead, understanding normal infant sleep often builds confidence, as it allows you to realize how normal your child's patterns actually are, as well as the temporary nature of this frequent nighttime waking. Plus, learning more gives you some well-researched ammunition to fire back at a questioning family member or friend!

Evidence-based research about infant sleep shows the following:

- From birth to three months, infants sleep between 15 and 17 hours every 24-hour period.
- Babies have a 90-minute rhythm. After being awake for 90 minutes, a baby will typically be sleepy again.
- At one month, most babies wake three or four times during the night.
- At two months, most babies wake two or three times during the night.
- At four months, most babies wake one or two times during the night.
- Night wakings are normal for babies and temporarily increase during developmental milestones such as rolling over, teething, crawling, walking, and so on.

- Most babies (70 to 80 percent) will sleep nine to 12 hours consecutively each night by nine months.

If your baby's night wakings are causing you anxiety, stress, or depression, consider a few options:

- Ask your partner if he or she would be willing to take over one night feeding a few times per week. Pump before you go to bed, and have your partner offer the bottle at the next feeding session.
- If you have the financial resources, consider hiring a postpartum doula who can bring your baby to you to breastfeed and take care of your baby in between night feedings.
- Ask your pediatrician or a sleep coach for strategies to promote healthy sleep for your baby during the daytime, as this often helps with sleep in the night as well. Sleep begets sleep.
- Speak with a postpartum therapist who can determine the underlying causes of the stress—whether it's fatigue or something more, like postpartum depression and anxiety— and provide guidance and support to ensure the emotional well-being you deserve.

I am a breastfeeding expert, not a sleep-training expert. As a mom, I know how exhausting those first several months are. We put our baby's needs before our own. While it's totally normal for babies to wake once or twice at four, five, and even six months of age, it can become tiresome for parents. If you and your partner decide for your own wellness that sleep assistance is important, there are many books and professionals you can turn to for specific advice. Remember, these night wakings are temporary, but definitely seek help if you feel like you are struggling due to lack of sleep.

COSLEEPING WITH A BREASTFED BABY

While a good number of parents don't go into parenthood planning to cosleep with their baby right away, many end up doing it to help everyone get the most sleep possible. Your baby can breastfeed lying next to you, and you don't even have to get out of bed. Plus, babies tend to sleep more soundly when in close proximity to their parents. If you want to cosleep safely, it is important to follow these guidelines:

You and your partner must be

- Nonsmokers
- Sober (from drugs, alcohol, or medications that make you drowsy)

Your baby must be

- Full-term and healthy
- Breastfeeding
- Kept on her back when not nursing
- Unswaddled, in light pajamas

You all need to be

- On a safe, flat surface (only adults may use a pillow and lightweight blanket)

If you like having Baby close to you at night but are uncomfortable with cosleeping, consider placing her in a Moses basket in your bed or in a bassinet connected to or at arm's reach from your bed.

Frequently Asked Questions

IS IT POSSIBLE TO HAVE TOO MUCH MILK?

Yes! Some moms produce more milk than their baby needs. This isn't always a problem. Some babies just gain a lot of weight, which is totally fine. Other babies become uncomfortable with the excess milk, which can cause gas and tummy discomfort. If you have an oversupply, you could pump a few times a day and store your milk in the freezer or donate to a mom in need. If you'd like to temper down your oversupply, some remedies include block feeding (feeding from one breast per feeding), leaning back while breastfeeding, and drinking a daily cup of of sage and mint tea.

WHY ARE MY BABY'S POOPS GREEN?

Baby's poop can be green for several reasons. First, babies have green poops as they transition from meconium to a more yellow, seedy poop in the first few days of life. Second, if you or your baby has to take antibiotics, it can cause belly discomfort and colored mucus in the poop or diarrhea. Third, Baby may be getting only foremilk (the more watery first milk) due to Mom's oversupply or perhaps Baby's ineffective feeding. Fourth, this could be a sign of a food intolerance.

I'VE HAD BREAST SURGERY. WILL I BE ABLE TO BREASTFEED?

Yes! Many women who have a history of breast surgery are able to breastfeed. Breast surgeries, such as augmentation and reduction, do create a higher risk for lower milk supply due to the breast tissue being changed and sometimes cut. Therefore, for the first few weeks after your baby is born, keep a close watch on your baby's weight gain to make sure he is getting enough and that your milk supply continues to increase to meet his needs.

Breastfeeding Through Changes

Nursing gives you superhuman powers.
How else could I be doing all this when
I'm usually a sleepaholic?

—GWEN STEFANI

Returning to Work/ Time Away

It's amazing how much more fun life gets when your baby turns three months old! He is now the life of the party, socially smiling rather than smiling because of gas. He is constantly trying to make eye contact with you so you will smile and talk to him, and he flirts right back with you. He now has a more predictable eating and sleeping pattern, making it easier for you to get out of the house and do things with friends and family. The "fourth trimester" is over, and things just start to feel easier. It is at around three months that many moms return to work or just feel more comfortable occasionally spending time away from their baby. This chapter will help you prepare for these separations, both practically and emotionally.

Revisiting Your Breastfeeding Goals

Whether you return to work when your child is six weeks, three months, or 12 months old, by that time you'll have established a breastfeeding pattern at home. This pattern will change once you return to work, but it can definitely be manageable with some advance planning. Returning to work should not sabotage your original breastfeeding goals, as there are laws in place to protect you, as well as a ton of books and websites that discuss creative ways to make pumping work for you while you are away from your baby. Take some time to revisit your original breastfeeding goals so you can assess and troubleshoot any obstacles that might come your way. Planning ahead can make all the difference!

Working and Breastfeeding

So many questions come to mind when returning to work: *How will I keep up my milk supply for my baby? When and where will I pump? Will my boss and coworkers be supportive of my pumping breaks or be difficult to work with?* Lack of employer support and the inability to pump frequently enough during the workday can certainly affect how long a mom will continue to breastfeed after she returns to work. Women who return to work are less likely to breastfeed for six months or a year compared to women who don't return to work. Challenges can include lack of access to a private place to pump, not enough break time, an ineffective pump, scheduling issues, and lack of a supportive environment. These trials can seem difficult to overcome, but we'll explore many ways in which you can proactively break down these barriers. In this chapter, you'll learn how to set yourself up for success by anticipating any challenges that may arise and employing solutions before they become huge problems.

Planning Ahead

Let's talk about planning ahead and assessing any potential obstacles or challenges. First, if you are currently having any challenges with breastfeeding, pumping, or getting your baby to take a bottle, seek some assistance while you're still home so you'll be ready for a smooth transition back to work.

Schedule a meeting with your boss or someone from your human resources department while still on maternity leave. Find out now how you can work together to maintain a manageable pumping schedule without impacting your work. You can come up with some creative solutions, if necessary, well before your first day back. In the United States, federal law states that employers with over 50 employees are required to provide "reasonable break time for an employee to express breastmilk for her nursing child for 1 year after the child's birth each time such employee has need to express the milk." Employers are also required to provide "a place, other than a bathroom, that is shielded from view and free from intrusion from coworkers and the public, which may be used by an employee to express breastmilk."

For those who work for an employer with fewer than 50 employees, this law doesn't protect you, but this is a good launching point to negotiate the standards your company can and should strive to have.

Figure out your caregiver situation. Will you work from home, will a partner/family member/nanny take care of your baby, or will your kiddo go to daycare? Find out how your intended caregiver wants you to leave your pumped milk: frozen or in the refrigerator, in bags or already portioned out into separate bottles? Will there be a backup supply of frozen milk in case of emergency?

Keep an extra stash of supplies in your pumping bag. This extra stash should include replaceable membranes, batteries (if necessary), extra pumping pieces, and a robust supply of snacks. Also, keep an extra shirt in your office just in case you spill milk down the front of the one you are wearing and need a wardrobe change.

Purchase a bag with reusable ice packs. This will allow you to store your pumped milk and keep it cool until you can put it in the refrigerator back at home.

Pick up a hands-free pumping bra. This is a lifesaver! You can pump, eat lunch, and answer e-mails (or look at videos of your baby) all at the same time! Genius!

> JUST THE FACTS
> Breastfeeding is associated with higher productivity and lower absenteeism for breastfeeding mothers.
> —*AMERICAN JOURNAL OF PUBLIC HEALTH*

Having a Stash

If you peruse the social media accounts of friends or acquaintances, you will undoubtedly find photos of freezers completely filled with bags of pumped milk, causing you to immediately panic over how you will get that much into your own freezer before you return to work. Let me put your mind at ease. That amount of frozen milk is not the norm, nor should it be your expectation. A great goal would be to have about 30 ounces of pumped milk in your freezer, that is, about two to three days' worth of frozen milk, just in case you need it. Remember, you'll also be pumping while you're at work to replace the milk your baby drinks while he's away from you. To get those 30 ounces in your freezer, start to pump after one morning breastfeeding session, a few days a week to daily. Since your baby will just have breastfed, you might get out an additional 1/2 ounce or 1 ounce each time. Once you have accumulated 3 or 4 ounces over a few days, put all that milk in a breastmilk freezer bag or container and freeze it. If you can put one or two bags in the freezer each week, you'll be set for when you return to work.

Knowing Where to Pump

Knowing where you will pump is an important topic to discuss with your boss and/or human resources before returning to work. As mentioned, if you don't have a private office, your employer (in a company of more than 50 employees) needs to designate a private space to pump, and it cannot be a bathroom. Some offices have designated pumping rooms, which, if shared with other pumping moms, should have a sign-up so pumping times can be coordinated among everyone using that space. Other offices have storage closets or unused office spaces that are converted into temporary pumping rooms. If you commute between several locations, learning to pump in the car can be time efficient and convenient. You can pump while you commute, or arrive at your location 15 minutes beforehand to pump once you park. Some moms choose to pump in their cars with the air-conditioning and favorite tunes blasting. See Resources (page 134), for more on creative pumping spaces.

Scheduling Pumping Times

Your pumping schedule will be determined by the age of your baby and how many hours you'll be away from her. If your baby is relying solely on your milk and hasn't started solids, you will want to pump every two to three hours, for about 15 minutes each time. Pumping both breasts at the same time can maximize efficiency. If you are away from your baby for eight to 10 hours, you can pump once on a lunch break and then a few hours both before and after. As your baby gets older and starts to take in more solid foods, you can probably drop down to two pumping sessions per day. Keep in mind you don't have to pump on the same schedule that your baby gets a bottle. Nor do you have to pump at the same time every day—your baby eats at different times each day when breastfeeding, too. So, remain flexible with your pumping schedule to allow for meetings and appointments that may differ in time throughout the week. For moms who work in a non-office environment, discuss with your boss ways to ensure you get enough break time by having your coworkers overlap during that small part of your shift.

Scheduling Feedings

You may find that your breastfeeding schedule and your pumping and bottle-feeding schedule away from your baby look very different. Some breastfeeding sessions will still last 30 minutes, and others will be a quick snack. Time in between breastfeeding sessions may still vary from day to day and night to night. Yet, your baby may be on a more predictable schedule when bottle-feeding with the caregiver, as oftentimes nannies and daycare providers feed more by schedule than on demand. There is no reason for you to try to mimic your baby's bottle-feeding schedule when breast-feeding on your days off, or to pump on your baby's bottle-feeding schedule. Your body is used to these variations. Plus, your baby will

A Mom's Story
CINDA

I'm an active-duty navy officer and mother of two girls. My journey to becoming a working, breastfeeding mother started almost four years ago with the birth of my first daughter.

Day 1 back at work, I found myself with no place to pump breast-milk. For months, I pumped anywhere that would provide some sense of privacy and still allow me to complete work requirements, which typically was in the bathroom or in my car. It was far from ideal and was super stressful. The biggest challenge was trying to coordinate pumping between meetings that, for the most part, I didn't have a lot of control over scheduling.

In the military culture, it can be intimidating to ask your supervisor for permission to do things outside of the norm or what's expected. I know that the navy is keenly interested in retaining females so they rise in the ranks of leadership. Advocating for breastfeeding is one step in the right direction to retain mothers in the military. After several months of making do, a fellow military breastfeeding mother and I set out on a journey to have our commands come into compliance with current navy breast-feeding instructions and guidance. This meant that our command was required to provide a room that wasn't a bathroom space, with privacy, a locking door, a refrigerator/freezer, outlets, and furniture. It also allowed for time to pump milk that would accommodate what the mother would need to maintain her supply. It was a long process, but by the time I left my command, there were five mother's rooms set up for breastfeeding mothers to pump milk with a multi-user pump.

I pumped for two years for my first daughter. She will be four this fall and breastfeeds right along with my infant. I hope that through my efforts, I can help other military mothers achieve the success that they envision for breastfeeding their children, whether it be for days or years.

navigate these variables with ease as she gets used to them, so keep doing what works best for the two of you when breastfeeding and pumping.

A Day in the Life

Creating a pumping plan can help paint an overview of what your day will look like. Here is a sample breastfeeding/pumping schedule for a mom who works eight hours and commutes to and from work.

6:30 A.M.	Breastfeed Baby
7:30 A.M.	Commute to work
8:00 A.M.	Start work
9:30 A.M.	First 15-minute pumping session
12:00 NOON	Second 15-minute pumping session (at lunch)
2:30 P.M.	Third 15-minute pumping session
5:00 P.M.	Leave work
5:30 P.M.	Breastfeed Baby
	Continue to breastfeed on Baby's regular schedule throughout the night

Now let's create your own customized pumping plan.

1. Write down the times you leave for work and get home.

2. Add a pumping session for when you typically take your lunch break.

3. Add a time that is between when you typically breastfeed your baby before work and your lunchtime pumping break (like at 9:30 a.m. in the sample).

4. Add a time that is between lunch and when you get home for your afternoon pumping session (like at 2:30 p.m. in the sample).

If you have a long commute, you could also consider pumping in the car before work. Of course, try this while driving in your neighborhood first before getting on the highway! If you drive to different locations throughout the day, pumping as you drive can absolutely be an option, as well as arriving at your location 15 minutes early to pump in the parking lot. Sometimes you just have to get creative!

The first few weeks will have a learning curve, but you'll find your routine fairly quickly.

First Week Back at Work

That first week back at work can feel funky. You might feel a whole slew of emotions. Some moms feel eager and happy to return to work. Having adult conversations that don't revolve around the topics of sleep and baby poop can feel exhilarating. Some moms feel sadness about leaving their baby on a daily basis. Some moms feel anxious about fitting in pumping and trying to keep up their milk supply while away from their baby. Most moms feel a combination of several emotions. It's so important to respect and honor the multitudes of emotions you are feeling, as they are normal and to be expected. As you and your baby settle into this new routine, you will find that it gets easier and more predictable. To get through this first week, try to take one day at a time. Look at videos of your baby while on your pumping breaks. And remember, nothing is better than coming home to your child who is eagerly waiting for you to return for snuggles and bonding.

THE BOTTLE STRIKE

While many moms worry that their baby will stop breast-feeding after being given a bottle, some babies actually refuse to take a bottle. This can be distressing to a mom about to go back to work, who is relying on her baby to take her pumped milk in a bottle while she is away. Bottle rejection or a bottle strike can happen for several reasons:

1. Baby has become so emotionally attached to the breast that she refuses to latch onto anything that feels different. To prevent this, introduce the bottle to your baby between three and six weeks old and then continue to offer it a few times a week so it becomes part of the feeding routine.

2. Baby has a sensitive gag reflex, so the bottle makes her choke, cough, or gag. This is often coupled with Baby having a high palate. To remedy this, look for bottles with shorter nipples and wider bases that don't go as far into Baby's mouth. Also, consider taking your baby for craniosacral or occupational therapy to relax her sensitive gag reflex.

3. Baby has a tongue tie (see page 47) that is preventing her from being able to cup her tongue around the narrow bottle nipple. To remedy this, consider having your baby's tongue tie released, and try new bottles with differently shaped nipples to see if she can grasp onto another more easily.

If your baby has taken a bottle before and is newly protesting the bottle, there is a very good chance that she will be willing to take a bottle after a few days of your being gone for more than a few hours. Those first few days back to work might be challenging for her, but typically she will eventually give in when she is really hungry.

How to Keep Your Caregiver from Overfeeding Your Baby

Pumping at work takes dedication, time, and stamina, and it can be frustrating to discover that meanwhile, your caregiver is offering way too much pumped milk to your baby. It can become impossible to keep up when Baby is being overfed. Here are some things to keep in mind:

- Try to calculate how much your baby needs per bottle, and leave bottles with that amount ready to serve. Babies over 13 pounds eat about 30 ounces every 24 hours. If your baby is eating seven times per day, he needs about 4 ounces per feeding or bottle. For babies under 13 pounds, take your baby's weight and multiply that by 2.5. Then divide that by the number of times your baby feeds in a 24-hour period. For example, a 10-pound baby who eats eight times in 24 hours will need 25 ounces in 24 hours ($10 \times 2.5 = 25$ ounces). According to this math, your baby would need about 3 ounces for each feeding or bottle.
- Teach your caregiver how to use paced bottle-feeding methods (see page 78), which slows down the feeding process. When a baby feeds quickly he tends to overeat, as his belly has not communicated with his brain to let him know he is full. Kind of like us on Thanksgiving! Slowing down bottle-feeding can prevent overeating and help your baby feel satisfied after finishing the bottle.
- Discuss with the caregiver ways to soothe your baby beyond the bottle. Your caregiver doesn't have magically soothing boobs, so suggest other ways to keep your baby happy, like taking Baby on a walk, going outside, rocking to sleep, babywearing, playing gentle music you know he likes, and more.

BREASTFEEDING AND TRAVELING FOR BUSINESS

For the mom who travels for work, here are some practical tips to keep up your milk supply while out of town:

- If you have the opportunity, pump a few extra times a day for at least two weeks before you leave on your business trip. This will build a surplus in your freezer for when you are away.

- Call your hotel before you leave home to request a refrigerator in your room.

- Bring a few zippered, insulated cooler bags, along with several ice packs to keep your pumped milk fresh during work hours. Transfer the milk to the hotel refrigerator when you get back to your room. Your milk will stay fresh for five to seven days in the hotel refrigerator.

- Use these insulated bags and ice packs when storing milk for your trip home. Just pack it in your checked luggage so you can bring home all that liquid gold without having to lug it through security.

- Try to pump every few hours, and once at night if your baby is still breastfeeding in the middle of the night, to keep your milk supply robust for when you get home. If your meetings are in a conference center or hotel, ask the concierge if there is a room that you can use (not a bathroom) to have some privacy while pumping. Aim to pump for about 15 minutes, which is about as long as it takes your coworkers to enjoy a coffee break.

Frequently Asked Questions

WHY DOES MY EXPRESSED BREASTMILK SMELL STRANGE?

If your pumped milk smells sour or soapy, first make sure that you are using proper storage and freezing guidelines. If you are following those guidelines, you might have excess lipase. Lipase is an enzyme that breaks down milk fat. If your milk has excess lipase, your milk may begin to smell funky anywhere from a few hours to a few days after it is pumped. If you notice this change of smell in your milk, you can scald it to deactivate the lipase and keep your milk drinkable for your baby. See Resources (page 134) for links to websites that explain excess lipase and how to scald your milk.

MY PUMP BROKE. WHAT SHOULD I DO?

If you are at work, hand express to keep yourself comfortable. Next, call the pump company, as most have a one-year warranty and will replace it for you, hopefully very quickly. Meanwhile, consider purchasing a hand pump as a backup until your new pump arrives.

I'M NOT PUMPING ENOUGH MILK AT WORK, BUT I KNOW MY SUPPLY IS FINE. WHAT SHOULD I DO?

Make sure your pump flanges fit appropriately and that the suction hasn't diminished with use. Flanges that are too tight or too small can make it more difficult for your milk to come out. Many lactation consultants can check this for you. Replace the tubing and any flexible pump pieces. Massage your breasts before putting on the pump as well as while pumping, as your hands can massage some hard-to-reach milk ducts better than the pump suction can. Hand express for a few minutes after pumping to eke out whatever is left in there. Consider pumping once a day on your days off and/or before you go to bed, just to get a few extra ounces per week.

MY MILK SUPPLY DIPPED WHEN I WENT BACK TO WORK. HOW CAN I INCREASE IT?

Try to have a glass of water and a nutrient-dense snack every time you sit down to pump, as not eating 2,000 calories per day and not drinking enough water can decrease your milk supply. Consider adding in another pumping session each day. Rent a hospital-grade pump for better pumping suction. Certain foods, herbs, and medications can help boost your milk supply (see Resources, page 134). Breastfeed your baby as often as she is willing on your days off and at night.

WHAT ARE SOME TIPS FOR EASING THE TRANSITION BACK TO WORK?

Get help with any breastfeeding or bottle-feeding challenges before you go back to work. Try to start back in the middle of the week to ease the transition. Meet with your boss or human resources while on maternity leave to work out pumping details. Bring an extra shirt that matches most of your outfits, just in case of a milk-spilling incident. Remember to take one day at a time; if your pumping schedule or output gets messed up one day, things should be easier the next. Talk to a coworker who has done this before to get tips for your personal working environment. Pack your pumping bag and your baby's daycare bag (if needed) before you go to bed so it's ready to go the next morning.

A Mom's Story
KATIE

I had truly excellent luck when it came to breastfeeding: minimal pain, a plentiful supply, and a baby with a good latch and a hearty appetite. Over the fourteen weeks of my maternity leave, I had plenty of hard times, but the hours I spent feeding my hungry son were a source of warmth and bonding, not stress.

By the time I was due to return to work, I figured it'd be easy enough adjusting to the new routine. I'd been pumping here and there all along so my husband could give our son an occasional bottle, and it didn't seem so difficult. And my company provided a decent space to pump—not all moms are so fortunate!

After about a week back at work, it was clear that my expectations had been a little too rosy. I rushed to find time to pump between meetings, and felt an immense amount of stress being away from my desk just as I was trying to get established in a new office. I spent countless pumping sessions with my laptop balanced on my knees, struggling to type with all of the pump paraphernalia in my way. And for all that, I never made quite as much milk as my ravenous baby seemed to drink—my carefully hoarded freezer stash dwindled day by day.

But as the months went by, the routine got easier and more predictable. I started to let go of the fear that my supply wouldn't be able to keep up. What mattered was that I was still able to breastfeed my baby boy every day, and he was growing huge and adorable. As long as I didn't stress myself out by expecting perfection, what I actually had was pretty great.

Parents are responsible for the *what*, *when*, and *where* of *feeding*; children are responsible for the *how much* and *whether* of *eating*.

—ELLYN SATTER, AUTHOR OF *CHILD OF MINE: FEEDING WITH LOVE AND GOOD SENSE*

STAGE 4

Introducing Solid Food

On to the next chapter in your breastfeeding journey: introducing solids! Cue adorable photos and videos of your baby smashing sweet potato and spaghetti all over her face, in her hair, and all over the highchair table. If your dog has been less than excited about sharing his home with your bundle of joy, his love will return once he realizes that your bubbly, bouncing baby is also his new source of delicious people food. For the next several months, you will help your baby experience and explore new flavors, tastes, and textures; at first, of course, as much of this new food will end up on her hands and the floor as in her mouth. Solids do not have to be considered a main food source until your baby is closer to a year. Until then, your breastmilk can continue to be the main component of your baby's nutrition. So, let's dive into the exciting topic of introducing solids!

Signs of Readiness

The American Academy of Pediatrics, World Health Organization, UNICEF, and several other health organizations recommend that all babies be breastfed for the first six months of life (no cereal, juice, or other foods) and that parents begin to complement breastmilk with solid foods starting at six months and older. There are several reasons for these recommendations. It takes about six months for your baby's gut to close and produce antibodies to coat his digestive tract, preventing illness and allergic reactions. Also, most babies are not developmentally ready for solids until at least six months.

Look for these signs of readiness for solids:

- Baby can sit up on his own without support—this will prevent choking.
- Baby is able to pick up items with a "pincer" grasp (between his thumb and forefinger).
- Baby shows interest in your meals and tries to grab food and put it in his mouth.

Not all babies meet all three of these readiness signs at six months, and that is okay. Breastmilk has all of the nutrients your baby needs until he is 12 months old, so it is recommended to hold off on introducing solids until your baby is completely ready.

How to Introduce Solid Foods

Since solids are meant to complement breastmilk for the first year rather than be a main source of nutrition, it is recommended that a mom breastfeed or offer breastmilk by bottle before offering solids at a feeding session. Think of solid foods as dessert. They are not needed at every meal. They are fun and delicious but can usually be served on an almost full stomach. Offering solids after breast-milk will also help protect your milk supply, allowing your baby to breastfeed as often as needed and keep up the demand for your breastmilk production. Your baby will still need about 30 ounces of breastmilk per day until he is about one year old.

For the first month or so after starting solids, offer your baby a serving (1 or 2 tablespoons) of solids per day, but don't stress if you skip days here and there. Meals can be about exploration rather than consumption. Offer just one food for a few days in a row to ensure that your baby doesn't show signs of an allergic reaction. Then move on to the next food. Some great introductory foods are puréed or mashed avocado, sweet potatoes, apples, bananas, and strained, puréed meat mixed with breastmilk. After a month or two, your baby will become more comfortable with the flavors and textures of solid foods—this is a great time to increase variety, amount, and frequency.

JUST THE FACTS

Breastfeeding exposes your baby to many different tastes. Formula has one taste. But through your breastmilk, your baby eventually gets a slight taste of whatever you eat, although not directly. This will later make introducing solid foods easier.

—OFFICE ON WOMEN'S HEALTH,
US DEPARTMENT OF HEALTH AND HUMAN SERVICES

NO INTEREST IN FOOD?

Some babies fall in love with solid foods right away, while others are completely uninterested for several months. Some babies like a particular food for a couple of weeks and then start to spit it out every time you offer it. Some babies prefer purées, while others prefer those foods that they can pick up on their own. Since the goal of introducing solids is exploration, allow your baby to use all of his senses to experience the smells, flavors, and textures of these new foods. Babies need to feel foods in their mouths and on their hands. What ends up on your baby's hands will most likely end up in your baby's mouth, which is an immersive way for him to examine and discover these new foods.

If your baby is truly showing no interest in solid foods as he gets close to one year old and is actually upset or repulsed by them, speak with your pediatrician who can determine the reasons behind this and recommend a specialist if necessary.

A Sample Feeding and Nursing Schedule

Introduction and frequency of solid-food meals will be determined by you and your baby. Here is a sample feeding and nursing schedule for a baby who is showing signs of readiness and interest in solids at six months. You will typically increase the amount and frequency of solid-food meals as your baby gets older; however, if your baby is not interested in increasing his intake of solids, that is totally fine, as well. Follow his lead and continue providing him with the recommended amount of breastmilk until his interest for solids increases.

6 TO 7 MONTHS

- Breastfeed or bottle-feed throughout the day—30 ounces of breastmilk
- One or two puréed or mashed meals per day (1 to 2 tablespoons each) after breastmilk

8 TO 9 MONTHS

- Breastfeed or bottle-feed throughout the day—30 ounces of breastmilk
- Two or three puréed, mashed, or lumpy meals per day (2 to 4 tablespoons each) after breastmilk

10 TO 11 MONTHS

- Breastfeed or bottle-feed throughout the day—30 ounces of breastmilk
- Three chunky, chopped meals per day (3 to 4 tablespoons each) after breastmilk

12 TO 24 MONTHS

- Breastfeed or cup feed throughout the day—no particular recommended amount
- Three meals and two or three snacks per day with varied servings of grains, vegetables, fruits, protein, and dairy
- At 12 months, feel free to offer solids before or after breastmilk

Frequently Asked Questions

WHAT IS BABY-LED WEANING?

When Americans hear the word *weaning*, we immediately think "giving up breastfeeding." In England, where Gill Rapley (the woman who coined the term "baby-led weaning") lives, *weaning* means "adding complementary foods." In baby-led weaning, babies feed themselves with age-appropriate foods that they can pick up with their own fingers. There are no purées, and cutlery is optional until the baby is able to hold a spoon or fork on his own. This is one method you can use to introduce solids.

WHEN IS A GOOD TIME TO INTRODUCE ALLERGENIC FOODS?

In 2013, the American Academy of Pediatrics reported on new data that suggested the early introduction of highly allergenic foods may reduce the risk of food allergy. Highly allergenic foods can be given as complementary foods once a few nonallergenic complementary foods have already been tolerated. Allergenic foods should initially be given at home rather than at daycare or a restaurant. Certain situations call for consultation with an allergist to discuss food introduction, including, among other issues, when an infant has poorly controlled severe atopic dermatitis despite treatment or has a reliable history of reacting immediately to a food.

Weaning from Breastfeeding

If anything else woke up every 45 minutes during the night demanding to see my wife's breasts, you kill it.

—RYAN REYNOLDS

STAGE 5

When It's Time
to Wean

· ·

Congratulations on getting this far in your breastfeeding journey! No doubt there were some ups and downs along the way, but you made it. Your baby received your liquid gold, and her body, her heart, and her immune system send you a huge THANK YOU! If you are about to delve into this chapter, let's assume it's because you are about to get curious about weaning your child. Clearly, every mom goes through the weaning process; we have no intentions of breastfeeding our children into college—although some may joke about that! It is completely normal to have mixed emotions about the weaning process. Most likely this has been an emotion-filled journey, and you might feel both excited and sad to have this time come to an end. No matter when you decide to wean, this chapter will provide you with some concrete steps on how to make this process as easy, both physically and emotionally, as possible for you and your child.

When to Wean?

Many factors influence when a mom decides to wean. Maybe you have met your breastfeeding goal and feel ready to wean. Maybe you've gone back to work and feel like pumping is not working for you. Maybe your child is starting to show less interest in breast-feeding, and you feel like it's a good time to follow his lead. Maybe you are not enjoying breastfeeding anymore and feel like you'd enjoy time with your child more if you didn't continue. Maybe you are trying to get pregnant again or are already pregnant and don't want to tandem nurse. Regardless of your reason, many moms have felt the same way that you do, which is why there is not one particular time to wean. The process looks different depending on the age of your child, but the reasons resonate with every breast-feeding mom.

> **JUST THE FACTS**
> Natural weaning occurs as the infant begins to accept increasing amounts and types of complementary feedings while still breastfeeding on demand. When natural weaning is practiced, complete weaning usually takes place between two and four years of age.
> —*PAEDIATRICS & CHILD HEALTH*

Preparing Emotionally

Depending on your reason for weaning, you might be feeling a range of emotions. If you are feeling super ready to wean, you might feel excited and anxious to get the process started. If breast-feeding has been a long, complicated journey, you might feel sad about the end of all the hard work you put in to get to this place, or you might feel like you tried everything and now it is time to move on. When your child initiates the weaning process, it may come as a relief if you are ready or heartbreaking if you planned to breastfeed for longer. These feelings are all expected and normal.

Finding ways to connect with your child other than breastfeeding will be really helpful during this time. Know that this process doesn't have to happen overnight, and it can take a few weeks to a few months—whatever feels right and helps you navigate this new stage in your relationship with your child. Be aware that weaning can trigger hormonal changes in your body as you start to shut down the milk-making factory, and some moms feel quite emotional during this process. Reach out for support if it feels overwhelming.

Weaning from Nighttime Feeds

Sometimes moms are not interested in completely weaning, but they want to wean from nighttime feedings. Night weaning can mean cutting out one feeding in the middle of the night or going the whole night without breastfeeding. Some babies will establish a sleeping pattern all on their own, sleeping long stretches throughout the night and essentially night weaning. This is more common for babies over nine months old, but it can happen sooner. If you are looking to night wean your child, here are a few things to keep in mind:

- If your baby is over six months old, is gaining weight appropriately and staying on her growth curve, and is breastfeeding or bottle-feeding well throughout the day, you might be able to start cutting out nighttime breastfeeding sessions. You'll want to do this slowly to make sure it doesn't cause your baby to stop gaining weight well.

- Night weaning can decrease a mom's milk supply, so if you feel like your supply has an unwanted dip, you might consider adding the night feeding back into your routine or pumping right before you go to bed.
- Night weaning can cause engorgement and plugged ducts if your breasts get too full, so cut out feedings slowly and mindfully so you stay as comfortable as possible.
- If your baby is not gaining weight well and is very distracted while feeding during the day, it is not recommended to night wean at this time. These night feedings might be the best ones she has during a 24-hour period, and cutting them out could cause her to gain less weight. Meeting with a lactation consultant can be helpful to determine how to get more sleep at night and help your baby breastfeed more efficiently during the day.
- If your baby is under six months old, it is not recommended to night wean, as it could have some negative effects on your baby's growth and your milk supply. If waking for night feedings is causing you significant emotional or physical distress, consider reaching out to a mental health professional to get support before the situation escalates. You might want to ask for help caring for your baby between night-feeding sessions, so you can literally just breastfeed and then go back to sleep. Also, mastering the side-lying position will help you get more rest during these night feedings. Finally, consider just pumping and having someone else bottle-feed your baby in the middle of the night if breastfeeding sessions take too long.

Weaning before 12 Months

If you wean your baby before she is 12 months old, you'll need to think about what additional liquid you'll offer her in place of your breastmilk. Until babies are 12 months old, they need about

30 ounces of breastmilk per day. If you don't have frozen milk to offer as you wean, you can choose between donor milk or formula to supplement. Typically, the weaning process happens in the following manner:

- Choose a particular feeding (like the 3:00 p.m. feeding) and replace that with a bottle of pumped milk or formula. Don't pump your breasts at this skipped feeding session.
- Skip this same feeding session every day so your body starts to slow down milk production.
- After a few days or a week (depending on how quickly you want to wean), your breasts shouldn't feel uncomfortable at this skipped feeding time anymore.
- Next, choose another feeding to eliminate. It is often recommended to choose a time that is not right before or after the feeding session you just dropped prior. For example, if you dropped the 3:00 p.m. feeding, next skip one in the middle of the night or in the morning.
- Again, skip this same feeding session every day so your body starts to slow down milk production.
- Wait until your breasts no longer feel full at this skipped feeding time before dropping another feeding session.
- Continue with this method until the weaning process is complete.

Most moms end up keeping the first morning breastfeeding session and the last one before bed as the final ones to wean from, as these are associated with some serious snuggle time.

Depending on your situation, you can choose between weaning slowly or more quickly. When weaning slowly, you might drop a feeding session every few days to a week, which means the weaning process could take about a month or two. When weaning quickly (over a week or two), you'll need to make sure that your breasts don't get too engorged during the process. To keep comfortable

BREASTFEEDING A TODDLER

The age range for breastfeeding a toddler is very wide, often ranging from about one to three years. There are many families who continue to breastfeed beyond toddlerhood, as their child enters preschool age. After the first year, breastfeeding still has incredible nutritional, immunological, and emotional value for your child, yet it's no longer the main source of nutrition for your toddler, except in extreme circumstances. Antibodies are still abundant in breastmilk, giving your toddler a second dose of immunity beyond what his own body is able to produce. Your milk is still jam-packed with nutrients such as fat; protein; vitamins A, B_{12}, and C; and calcium and folate. Toddlers also find so much comfort in breastfeeding. It's like you have magical calming serum streaming out of your body. Your toddler feels overwhelmed by a stressful, overstimulating situation? Pop him on the boob to take things down a notch. Your toddler falls down at the playground and bonks her head? Not much helps dry up tears like breastfeeding. And for those times when your kiddo has a cold or just a really bad day, snuggling up on Mom while nursing seems to make everything right in the world.

All that being said, when this elated feeling about breastfeeding is not so mutual anymore, and you want to explore other ways for your toddler to decompress and soothe, the recommendations in this chapter should make the weaning transition a smooth one.

when weaning quickly, you can drink sage or mint tea, wrap your breasts in refrigerated green cabbage, and take over-the-counter medications that dry up mucous membranes.

Weaning after 12 Months

Babies older than 12 months do not require a particular quantity of breastmilk per day, as they are usually eating lots of solid foods by this time. So, when weaning a toddler who's a year or older, there is no need to supplement with formula in place of breastmilk. Just serve your kiddo pumped milk (if you have it) or water in a cup with his meals. The process of weaning by dropping feedings over the course of a few weeks or months can look exactly the same as when weaning a baby under 12 months. However, your toddler might be adamant about wanting to breastfeed, which means you will need a few more strategies to support him emotionally.

One recommendation is called "don't offer, don't refuse." If your toddler doesn't ask to breastfeed, don't offer. If she wants to breast-feed, don't refuse. If you can anticipate that your child is going to want to breastfeed at a certain time, offer her something else to do. Consider distracting her with a favorite snack, a playdate with a friend, playtime outside, or a favorite book. If your child likes to breastfeed before naps or bedtime, replace this nursing session with another routine such as reading a story, singing to your child and relaxing in a rocking chair or bed (in a different location than where you breastfed before), or having your partner put your child to bed. Introduce a new "lovie," like a soft stuffed animal or blanket, for her to hold tightly while falling asleep. Once your child is fully weaned, you can celebrate your accomplishments with her, letting her know how proud you are of your shared journey.

Finding New Forms of Closeness

Many moms, even those who were eager to wean, miss the closeness that breastfeeding created between them and their child. However, there are countless ways to connect and bond with your child. This is just one of the many milestones in your family life, and it is important to celebrate Baby's growth and your collective success.

Just as your partner can find ways to bond with your baby, now it's your turn to explore new ways of experiencing closeness with your child. Here are some tips:

- Create new routines that replace nursing around bedtime. Snuggle in a rocking chair and sing lullabies, as you both unwind from your day.
- Find new activities that you both enjoy (depending on your child's age), both in and out of your home. Playdates with friends, exploring nature and your neighborhood, blowing bubbles, playtime with the dog, walks to the park—you've got a big world to introduce your child to!
- Babywearing is a great way to stay close, both physically and emotionally, before and after weaning, so consider investing in a carrier or wrap that feels good to both of you.
- Look on YouTube for infant massage videos. Massage is a wonderful tool to use to bond, especially when you or your child needs help decompressing from an overwhelming day.

NURSING DURING PREGNANCY

Getting pregnant while breastfeeding is absolutely possible and may raise questions in your mind about where to go to from here in your breastfeeding journey. Most women can definitely continue to breastfeed throughout their pregnancies. Most moms find that their nipples become much more sensitive while pregnant, sometimes causing them to wean their nursling due to the discomfort. Some children self-wean once Mom becomes pregnant, as milk supply tends to dip by mid-pregnancy, while other children don't seem bothered at all by the drop in milk supply.

If you continue breastfeeding, however, it is important to make sure you are eating enough calories to support your body, your milk supply, *and* your growing baby. You might read online that breastfeeding while pregnant can trigger contractions and miscarriages. No specific research has been conducted on this topic, but related research shows that a pregnant uterus is protected by elevated progesterone and natural oxytocin blockers, therefore not creating an increased risk for most pregnant breastfeeding moms. If you have a high-risk pregnancy, it's important to work with your health care provider and do more personal research to make the most educated choice for your situation and family.

If you end up breastfeeding throughout your entire pregnancy, your mature milk will turn back to colostrum between the fourth and eighth months of pregnancy. No worries—your breastfeeding child cannot deplete this, as you will continue to make colostrum until your milk turns back to mature breastmilk, a few days after your new baby is born. Your older breastfeeding child will most likely be very excited once your new baby is born, as the milk will become plentiful again!

Frequently Asked Questions

CAN I BRING BACK MY MILK SUPPLY IF I CHANGE MY MIND AND NO LONGER WANT TO WEAN?

Yes, but this can be quite challenging, depending on how dried up your milk supply is. Weaning slowly, by dropping a feeding/pumping session every four to seven days or even longer, will allow you some time to decide if you really want to completely wean or not. If you change your mind early on, bringing back your milk supply shouldn't be too difficult. Weaning quickly or changing your mind when you are almost completely dried up will take a big effort to boost your milk supply again.

WHAT SHOULD I DO WHEN MY WEANED CHILD SUDDENLY SEEMS INTERESTED IN BREASTFEEDING AGAIN?

It is not uncommon for a weaned child to start showing interest in breastfeeding again when a sibling is born or when he is going through a new transition and is looking for familiarity and comfort during this process. You have several options when your weaned child seems interested in breastfeeding again. One, you could just go with it and let your kiddo soothe himself by dry breastfeeding. This might last a few days to a few weeks, depending on what works best for you and your child. Two, you can tell your child that the milk is all gone, and come up with another satisfying way to meet his needs for soothing and comfort.

HOW LONG DOES IT TAKE FOR MILK TO DRY UP COMPLETELY?

After weaning completely, you may still be able to squeeze out a little milk for a couple of weeks or up to a year, depending on how long you breastfed and how quickly you weaned. Most moms find that they dry up within a couple of weeks, and their breasts begin to lose their "milk-producing" shape within a couple of months.

Breastfeeding Stories
from New Moms

One of my favorite quotes from a fellow mom is "We do not mother alone." While this book is filled with a plethora of information to guide you through your breastfeeding journey, it is the stories you hear from other moms and the stories YOU share with others that truly round out your experience. We are not meant to parent alone, which is why we need both professional advice, as well as a mama tribe. I wanted to close with a few additional personal stories that highlight varied experiences of breastfeeding mothers. Each story expands the notion of what it means to breastfeed successfully. My hope is that they provide you some initial support along your breastfeeding journey.

Aran

From the true definition, I do not "exclusively" breastfeed my baby. However, I do give my baby all the breastmilk that I have. But he needs more to be happy and healthy, so he also receives formula and, when he was very young, he received donor milk. Honestly, I am so tired of the "low supply" conversation, I wish there were a different word for how I feed my baby—a word that matches the pride of the mamas who exclusively breastfeed their little ones all that they produce.

Thinking about it, I have never been an exclusive type of person, and the opposite of exclusive is inclusive. I have *inclusively* breastfed my baby for nine months (way longer than I would have thought in the beginning!). This is the word that I am using to define my breastfeeding experience.

In the inclusive camp, mamas know the best and worst of both worlds. The best of breastfeeding includes the joys of nourishing your baby with your body and making personalized milk. Then there is the best of formula: the intervention that provides life-saving nutrition to support healthy growth and development. The worst of breast-feeding includes the sometime difficulties: mastitis, plugged ducts, yeast, blebs, and so on! For formula, besides the cost, the worst includes the bottles to be cleaned, sterilized, and cleaned again.

In the inclusive camp, the mamas are incredible as they work so hard to maintain their milk supply for their little ones while also accepting help in the form of formula or donor milk. It is not one way or the other; it is all the ways: the breastfeeding, the pumping, the supplementing, the love, the dedication, the tears and the sweat (especially on hot days)! It's the inclusiveness of the experience.

I don't want to use a breastfeeding definition that makes mamas feel bad that their milk supplies are low (I worked through that one) or for needing to use formula (I worked though that one, too). Saying that "I inclusively breastfeed" is so much more positive and empowering than saying, "I have low supply and need to supple-ment." My lactation consultant always said to me, "He is getting your milk." That has become my motto. The amount doesn't matter because he is getting my milk.

Rena

It was about 30 hours after my son was born, and things were going from bad to worse with breastfeeding. I knew the discharge plan of "just go to a free support group for help" wasn't going to cut it. I called a lactation consultant from the hospital to set up an appointment. She came to our house and spent time talking with us about our struggles and goals, set up a workable plan (not the crazy feed-and-pump-every-two-hours plan the hospital had us on), and also confirmed my gut instinct that the issues would take a few weeks to resolve. Over those few weeks, we attended her free support group, which was a great place to meet other moms having similar challenges, get advice, and check in on our baby's progress.

After a few weeks, we decided to have our baby's tongue tie clipped, and it was the best decision. My son went from barely gaining ½ ounce a day to gaining 1½ ounces a day, and the extreme pain I was having and blisters I had disappeared. After over a year of breastfeeding and pumping, I got to donate my extra 3,500 ounces of milk to a milk bank. That was truly my rainbow after the storm, something I never imagined I'd be able to do.

Natalie

Pregnancy and childbirth were so seamless and natural that I assumed breastfeeding would be the same. When my son was four days old, I took him to a lactation consultant. I wanted an evaluation of his latch to make sure we were on the right path. At this first appointment, I found out my son had lip and tongue ties. They weren't interfering with his feeding and I wasn't having pain, so we had no cause for concern.

After a month of poor weight gain, it appeared that my son's ties were actually causing challenges, so we had them released. Around the same time, I needed to increase my milk supply, so I started pumping, taking herbs, and feeding him with a supplemental nursing system. I also called my sister-in-law, who is a breastfeeding mom. She immediately came over with galactagogue-rich foods and tea, and even pumped her own breastmilk for my son while I built up my supply!

After a few weeks, my son is doing so much better. We were able to "graduate" from the supplemental nursing system, and his weight gain remains excellent without it. I've attended multiple support groups and lactation consultant visits. I am so thankful to live in my community, where there is access to numerous resources. We are only a few months into this journey, but I feel so much confidence and support moving forward.

Galit

After preterm labor at 23 weeks, and four months of bed rest, I had twin boys at 37 weeks and three days. They weighed 5.5 and almost 6 pounds (amazing!). I wanted nothing more than to provide for them and ensure their health. Breastfeeding started out pretty rough. My colostrum was hard to obtain, and milk took forever to come in. We were told to supplement with formula to keep them out of the NICU (they lost weight after birth, as all babies do), so we obliged. We went home with two healthy boys after four days!

For several months we dealt with painful feedings, plugged ducts, mastitis, thrush, vasospasms, and low milk supply. Our big milestone came at about three months: I realized the boys were being bottle supplemented with only *my* milk. I was finally producing enough to feed two growing boys, and we were off formula! Hooray! Eventually, supplementation was no longer necessary.

So, was all this craziness, frustration, and pain worth it? Heck, yes! In addition to their health being amazing, we get some great bonding time. I pet their heads, and they give me smiles, hold each other's hands, and sometimes giggle while nursing. At 8 1/2 months, they eat three solid-food meals a day now, and I nurse them five times a day as well. The enzymes, antibodies, and good stuff my milk provides for them are so important. We're learning, growing, and laughing so much every day. We've hit the latest "golden age" of our babies and are enjoying each moment. It's just amazing.

Cara

I never expected I might need anything more than my breasts to feed my baby. The reality is that my breastfeeding relationship with my baby included supplemental nursing systems, tubes, donor breastmilk, formula, pumps, tears, lactation consultations, herbal supplements, medications, support groups, and my breasts. Insufficient glandular tissue meant that my breasts never produced more than a quarter of my baby's daily nutritional needs. Surprised, confused, and devastated by my body's inability to provide all of her nutrition, I turned to other mothers for help. These moms offered nourishment from their bodies for my baby, generously and open-heartedly. Feeding my baby donated milk through a tube at my breast was soothing for my broken heart. When I was finally able to let go of the hope of my breasts providing enough breastmilk, I ceased the pumping, medications, herbs, and weighed feedings. My baby was eight months old, and the next 10 months were the sweetest times of our breastfeeding relationship. She nursed at my breasts and what came through the tube was sometimes donor milk, sometimes formula, and eventually, cow's milk. She never knew or noticed the difference, and she thrived from the nourishment that came through the tube and the nourishment that came from my embrace. I only wish that I had let it go sooner. Because when I finally let go and reimagined breastfeeding success, I thrived as a nursing mother. When my second was born, he came home to a freezer full of donated breastmilk from loving moms.

Michelle

In December 2013, my sweet baby girl arrived. She latched and we were a nursing team. Twenty-four hours later I was told she was Coombs positive and her jaundice levels were high. She was sleepy, she was losing too much weight, and I needed to give her formula in a bottle. I cried lots of tears. "Formula? No way!" But I had no other options. Every time I fed her, I felt awful and felt like I was letting her down. Seven days later I was told, "Your daughter is failure to thrive." Cue more tears, more formula, more guilt, and not a lot of milk being produced from me. Over the next month, my journey consisted of doctors' visits, pumping eight times a day, a baby screaming at the breast due to bottle preference and low supply, tube feeding, domperidone; and yet my milk never fully came.

Five weeks in, a friend asked me to go to a breastfeeding support group. I went and hoped no one would notice me feeding formula to my sweet baby who wouldn't latch more than five minutes. Everyone noticed, yet no one judged me. After a month, a mama whom I hardly knew asked if I wanted her to pump for me, and then another offered to help as well. This would begin my donor milk journey, and a mental shift in my head that allowed me to stop seeing what I wasn't capable of and start enjoying the beauty that came from a community that would end up feeding both of my babes! I threw away my pumping and tube-feeding schedule right along with the lies that told me I wasn't enough because I couldn't get my body to do what I needed to do to fully feed my baby. We kept nursing as much as possible and made it to 10 months with my first child and 16 months with my second.

Today I am working to become an IBCLC because of the non-judgmental support I received from our lactation consultants' community. They didn't sprinkle magic fairy breastfeeding dust on me that fixed all issues, but they gave me a plan that was doable. They gave me tools to accomplish the goals I set for myself. They gave me hope and provided me with a community that was there to cheer me on. When I think about my breastfeeding journey, it is less about feeding my children and more about the discovery that we mamas cannot mother alone; we were never intended to do so. It takes a village to raise a baby, and for me, it took a village to feed mine. I am forever grateful.

Elizabeth

I tried everything under the sun to give my baby my breastmilk. I tried to nurse him at first and when that didn't work out, I exclusively pumped for him. My baby had a weak suck and I had low milk supply. Later, I found out that I have IGT (insufficient glandular tissue), which meant my breasts never developed the appropriate amount of milk-producing tissue. It was both devastating and relieving to find out there was an actual medical reason for my difficulties.

When my son was two months old, I saw an offer for donor milk on a local mama-centered Facebook group, and I contacted the donor. I was terrified at the thought of the risks involved in trusting someone enough to give her milk to my precious baby. On the other hand, I was also elated at the thought of being able to give my baby the benefits of breastmilk, so ultimately, I decided to take the donation. My baby did very well with the milk, and so we continued to receive milk donations. Over 10 months, there were about 45 generous mamas who donated milk to us.

Not being able to breastfeed was one of the most traumatizing experiences of my life, but being the recipient of milk donations has been one of the most miraculous ones. I am so humbled by the generosity and selflessness of the donor moms.

Several years later, I was terrified of having the same struggles with breastfeeding my second baby, Chesa, so I prepared myself as best I could with a plan, a backup plan, and an understanding that I might have the same disappointments as last time. I'm thrilled to report that even though we had a rough start, Chesa is still nursing at six months old. We have had to minimally supplement with donor milk and formula using an SNS (supplemental nursing system) for most of her life, and we are fine with it. The experience of having my baby latch and get some milk from me is amazingly healing. I am so grateful for all the support we received that helped our journey have a happy ending.

Breastmilk Storage Guidelines

Here is a short list of guidelines for storing human breastmilk. These storage times assume you are feeding a full-term, healthy baby. Milk storage guidelines for a premature baby or a baby with a compromised immune system can be found at the website of the San Diego Breastfeeding Center (sdbfc.com) by searching "How long does my breast milk stay fresh?"

FRESHLY EXPRESSED MILK IN A ROOM 72°F OR COOLER	6 to 10 hours
INSULATED COOLER WITH ICE PACK	24 hours
REFRIGERATOR (FRESHLY PUMPED MILK)	3 to 7 days
REFRIGERATOR (PREVIOUSLY FROZEN MILK)	24 hours
SELF-CONTAINED FREEZER	6 months
DEEP FREEZER	12 months

Additional considerations

- Thaw frozen milk under cool water or in the refrigerator overnight.
- Warm milk in a bottle warmer, or immerse the bottle/bag in a container of warm water.
- Never microwave your pumped milk.

Glossary

alveoli: The small cavities or sacs found in the mammary gland.

antibody: Also called immunoglobulin, a protective protein produced by the immune system in response to the presence of a foreign substance, called an antigen. Antibodies recognize and latch onto antigens in order to remove them from the body.

areola: A small circular area, in particular, the ring of pigmented skin surrounding a nipple.

baby-led weaning: Term coined by Gill Rapley. *Weaning* means "adding complementary foods." In baby-led weaning, babies feed themselves with age-appropriate foods that they can pick up with their own fingers.

bilirubin: A compound produced by the normal breakdown of red blood cells. Normally, it passes through the liver, which releases it into the intestines as bile (a liquid that helps with digestion).

colostrum: The first milk from the mammary glands after giving birth, rich in antibodies.

craniosacral therapy: A system of alternative medicine intended to relieve pain and tension by gentle manipulations of the skull regarded as harmonizing with a natural rhythm in the central nervous system.

doula: An individual who is trained to assist a woman during childbirth and who may provide support to the family after the baby is born.

engorgement: Overfilling that occurs in the mammary glands due to expansion and pressure exerted by the synthesis and storage of breast milk.

finger-feeding: A method of giving a baby pumped milk or formula without using a bottle, when the baby needs supplementation. A feeding tube is attached to an adult's finger and syringe, and is then filled with pumped milk or formula. The baby gets this milk when sucking on the adult's finger, where the feeding tube is attached.

frenectomy: Also known as a frenulectomy or frenotomy, the removal of a frenulum, a small fold of tissue that prevents an organ in the body from moving too far or effectively.

galactagogue: An herb that is used to help increase breastmilk production in nursing mothers.

insufficient glandular tissue (breast hypoplasia): Also called underdeveloped breasts or tubular breasts, may contain very little breast tissue that can produce breast milk. Breast hypoplasia is something that a woman is born with, and as she grows, the breast tissue does not fully develop.

international board-certified lactation consultant (IBCLC): A health care professional who specializes in the clinical management of breastfeeding.

jaundice: A common condition in newborns that refers to the yellow color of the skin and whites of the eyes that happens when there is too much bilirubin in the blood.

lactation amenorrhea method (LAM): The natural postpartum infertility that occurs when a woman is not menstruating due to breastfeeding. LAM is only 98 percent effective as a birth control method if her baby is less than six months old, menstrual periods have not yet returned, and the baby is breastfeeding on cue both day and night and gets nothing but breastmilk or only token amounts of other foods.

lactation educator: A person who has taken a class about breastfeeding for 20 to 45 hours and has taken an exam.

lactogenic: Inducing the secretion of milk.

laid-back breastfeeding (biological nurturing): A breastfeeding position in which a mother leans back with all body parts well supported and her baby lies tummy down on Mom's semi-reclined body.

large for gestational age (LGA): An indication of high prenatal growth rate. LGA is often defined as a weight, length, or head circumference above the 90th percentile for that gestational age at birth.

latch: The way a baby takes the breast into his or her mouth.

late-preterm infant: An infant born at a gestational age between 34 0/7 weeks and 36 6/7 weeks.

letdown: Milk releasing from the milk ducts.

lipase: An enzyme that breaks down the fats in breastmilk to help a baby digest it.

mammary gland: An exocrine gland in mammals that produces milk to feed young offspring.

meconium: The earliest stool of a mammalian infant. Unlike later feces, meconium is composed of materials ingested during the time the infant spends in the uterus: intestinal epithelial cells, lanugo, mucus, amniotic fluid, bile, and water.

Montgomery glands: Sebaceous glands in the areola surrounding the nipple. The glands make oily secretions (lipoid fluid) to keep the areola and the nipple lubricated and protected.

oxytocin: A hormone produced by the pituitary gland in the brain. It increases relaxation, lowers stress and anxiety, lowers blood pressure, and causes muscle contractions. Oxytocin is also the hormone involved in social relationships, bonding, trust, and love.

paced bottle-feeding: A method of bottle-feeding that mimics breastfeeding. Paced feeding allows babies more control over their intake of breastmilk by responding to their cues and may also prevent postfeeding fussiness by reducing overfeeding.

plugged (or clogged) milk duct: A hard, tender swelling in the breast, which can vary in size from a pea to a peach and may feel painful while breastfeeding.

prolactin: A hormone produced by the pituitary gland in the brain, mainly used to help women produce milk after childbirth.

SIDS (sudden infant death syndrome): The unexplained death, usually during sleep, of a seemingly healthy baby less than a year old.

small for gestational age (SGA): A term used to describe a baby who is smaller than the usual size for the number of weeks of pregnancy. SGA babies usually have birth weights below the 10th percentile for babies of the same gestational age.

thrush: A medical condition in which a yeast-shaped fungus called *Candida albicans* overgrows in the mucous membranes.

tongue tie (tight frenulum): An unusually short, thick, or tight band of tissue that tethers the bottom of the tongue to the floor of the mouth.

weaning: The gradual replacement of breastfeeding with other foods and ways of nurturing.

Resources

Favorite breastfeeding websites

Instead of consulting Dr. Google at 3:00 a.m., bookmark all of these evidence-based, mother-supportive websites to get your breast-feeding questions answered.

- The Badass Breastfeeder: www.thebadassbreastfeeder.com
- Breastfeeding Basics: www.breastfeedingbasics.com
- DIY Breastfeeding: www.youtube.com/DIYbreastfeeding
- Dr. Jack Newman: www.breastfeedinginc.ca
- Kellymom: kellymom.com
- Nancy Mohrbacher: www.nancymohrbacher.com
- San Diego Breastfeeding Center: www.sdbfc.com/blog

Stage 1

RELIEVING ENGORGEMENT

When engorgement hits, these videos will provide you some hands-on ways to remove your milk easily and comfortably.

- Hand expression: https://youtu.be/i8BjLYpGd4M
- Stanford hand expression: med.stanford.edu, search "hand expressing milk"
- Therapeutic breast massage: bfmedneo.com/resources/videos

BREASTFEEDING POSITIONS

Additional visuals on how to latch your baby in different breast-feeding positions.

- DIY Breastfeeding: https://youtu.be/LFH6pezHqsE
- Laid-back breastfeeding: www.biologicalnurturing.com

PUMPING ADVICE

Pumping techniques, breast pump reviews, milk storage recommendations and more!

- Expressing Mama: expressing-mama.com

EATING TO SUPPORT BREASTFEEDING

"Baby brain" and limited time can make meal planning quite the challenge. Here are a few of my favorite books and websites with easy-to-make meals that support breast milk production.

Books

- *The First Forty Days: The Essential Art of Nourishing the New Mother* by Heng Ou
- *Nourishing Meals: 365 Whole Foods, Allergy-Free Recipes for Healing Your Family One Meal at a Time* by Alissa Segersten and Tom Malterre
- *Slow Cooker: The Best Cookbook Ever with More Than 400 Easy-to-Make Recipes* by Diane Phillips

Websites

- damndelicious.net
- exerciseandpregnancy.blogspot.com, search "Top 10 Foods to Include After Baby"
- Pinterest boards for Instant Pot, Whole30, sheet pan, Crock-Pot
- stupideasypaleo.com

STAGE 2

AT-BREAST SUPPLEMENTATION SYSTEMS

For moms who need to supplement their babies long term, these at-breast supplementation systems keep baby feeding from the breast while supplementing.

- Lact-Aid Nursing Trainer: www.lact-aid.com
- Medela Supplemental Nursing System: www.medelabreast feedingus.com, search "SNS"

BREAST HYPOPLASIA/INSUFFICIENT GLANDULAR TISSUE (IGT)

Fantastic resources for moms dealing with IGT.

- Facebook IGT group: www.facebook.com/groups/IGTmamas
- *Finding Sufficiency: Breastfeeding with Insufficient Glandular Tissue* by Diana Cassar-Uhl

INCREASING MILK SUPPLY

With so many techniques, herbs, and medications to choose from, here are some resources to start the breastfeeding journey with increasing milk supply.

- *Breastfeeding Mother's Guide to Making More Milk* by Diana West and Lisa Marasco
- Kellymom low milk supply info: kellymom.com/hot-topics/low-supply
- Lactogenic foods: www.mobimotherhood.org/lactogenic-foods-and-herbs.html
- Low Milk Supply: www.lowmilksupply.org
- MOBI Motherhood International: www.mobimotherhood.org

WITCHING HOUR

Tips for distinguishing between the witching hour and colic, as well as tips for surviving these few hours each night.

- San Diego Breastfeeding Center: www.sdbfc.com/blog , search "witching hours"
- San Diego Breastfeeding Center: www.sdbfc.com/blog , search "witching hour vs colic"

BREASTFEEDING/NURSING IN PUBLIC (NIP)

Breastfeeding in public shouldn't be anxiety provoking. With these resources, you will be a pro in no time at all!

- Badass Breastfeeder NIP course: www.thebadassbreastfeeder .com/become-a-badass-public-breastfeeder-in-7-days -introduction/
- List of NIP laws, state by state: www.ncsl.org/research/health /breastfeeding-state-laws.aspx
- San Diego Nursing in Public Task Force: www.sdbfc.com/nip

ALL-PURPOSE NIPPLE OINTMENT

Here's the recipe.

- www.breastfeedinginc.ca/informations/all-purpose -nipple-ointment-apno/

PACED BOTTLE-FEEDING

Websites offering breastfeeding-friendly bottle-feeding tips.

- Kellymom: kellymom.com/bf/pumpingmoms/feeding-tools /bottle-feeding
- Nurtured Child: blog.nurturedchild.ca/index.php/2010/12/10 /baby-led-bottle-feeding

BREASTFEEDING AFTER BREAST SURGERY

For moms who have had breast augmentation or reduction surgery, this book provides great insight into maximizing your breastfeeding success.

- *Defining Your Own Success: Breastfeeding after Breast Reduction Surgery* by Diana West

TONGUE TIES

Tongue ties can make breastfeeding more challenging. These websites provide detailed descriptions of tongue ties and what to do if they cause breastfeeding challenges.

- Dr. Ghaheri: www.drghaheri.com
- Kellymom: kellymom.com/health/baby-health/bfhelp-tonguetie

STAGE 3

PUMPING-AT-WORK LAWS

US laws that protect a breastfeeding mother when returning to work.

- Lactation accommodation federal law: www.dol.gov/whd/regs /compliance/whdfs73.htm

CREATIVE PUMPING SPACES FOR THE WORKING ENVIRONMENT

If you have a unique work environment or situation, this website offers creative solutions for pumping-at-work challenges.

- Office on Women's Health: www.womenshealth.gov/breastfeed ing/employer-solutions/common-solutions/solutions.html

GOING BACK TO WORK

Books, websites, and podcasts that offer tips and tricks for creating a pumping schedule, protecting your milk supply, and making sure your caregiver doesn't overfeed your baby while you are at work.

- kellymom.com/bf/pumpingmoms/pumping/bf-links-pumping
- *Work. Pump. Repeat.: The New Mom's Survival Guide to Breast-feeding and Going Back to Work* by Jessica Shortall
- www.newmommymedia.com/series/back-to-work
- www.sdbfc.com/working-moms
- www.workandpump.com

TRAVELING FOR WORK

Tips for pumping while traveling, as well as how to bring all of that precious milk home with you.

- www.sdbfc.com/blog/2012/5/29/how-can-i-keep-up-my-milk
-supply-while-on-a-business-trip.html
- www.sdbfc.com/blog/2015/5/20/top-6-tips-for-protecting-your
-milk-supply-while-traveling-f.html

EXCESS LIPASE

If your milk is turning sour quickly after pumping, here are resources to stop that from happening, including how to scald it.

- kellymom.com/bf/pumpingmoms/milkstorage/lipase
-expressedmilk
- www.sdbfc.com/blog/2012/9/4/battling-and-resolving-excess
-lipase-in-breastmilk.html
- www.sdbfc.com/blog/2012/4/25/why-does-my-milk-smell
-sour.html

BROKEN PUMP

Whom to contact if your breast pump kicks the bucket.

- www.sdbfc.com/working-moms/ FAQ section: My Pump Broke: What Do I Do?

STAGE 4

INTRODUCING SOLIDS

Books and websites with plentiful guidance for this next step.

- *The Baby-Led Weaning Cookbook* by Gill Rapley, PhD, and Tracey Murkett
- *Born to Eat* by Wendy Jo Peterson and Leslie Schilling
- *Fearless Feeding* by Jill Castle and Maryann Jacobsen
- Rapley Weaning: www.rapleyweaning.com
- *Super Nutrition for Babies* by Katherine Erlich and Kelly Genzlinger

STAGE 5

WEANING

Tips for when you and baby decide it's time.

- www.breastfeedingbasics.com/articles/weaning-your-baby
- kellymom.com/category/ages/weaning/wean-how

BREASTFEEDING WHILE PREGNANT

An article with valuable insight on this issue.

- kellymom.com/pregnancy/bf-preg/bfpregnancy_safety

References

American Academy of Pediatrics. "AAP Reaffirms Breastfeeding Guidelines." February 27, 2012. www.aap.org/en-us/about-the-aap /aap-press-room/pages/aap-reaffirms-breastfeeding -guidelines.aspx

American Academy of Pediatrics. "Breastfeeding and the Use of Human Milk." *Pediatrics* 129, no. 3 (March 2012). pediatrics .aappublications.org/content/129/3/e827

American Academy of Pediatrics. "Early Introduction of Allergenic Foods May Prevent Food Allergy in Children." *AAP News* 34, no. 2 (February 2013). www.aappublications.org/content/34/2/13

Black Bear, Jolie. "The Alphabet Soup of Breastfeeding Support." *Native Mothering.* Accessed November 28, 2017. nativemothering .com/2013/03/the-alphabet-soup-of-breastfeeding-support/

Buckley, Sarah. *Gentle Birth, Gentle Mothering: A Doctor's Guide to Natural Childbirth and Gentle Early Parenting Choices.* Berkeley, CA: Celestial Arts, 2008.

Cleveland Clinic. "Kangaroo Care." Accessed November 28, 2017. my.clevelandclinic.org/health/articles/newborn-kangaroo-care

Doan, T., Gardiner A., Gay, C. L., and Lee, K. A. "Breast-Feeding Increases Sleep Duration of New Parents." *Journal of Perinatal and Neonatal Nursing* 21, no. 3 (July–September 2007): 200–206. www.ncbi.nlm.nih.gov/pubmed/17700096

Doucleff, Michaeleen. "What Moms Need to Breast-Feed: Chicken Soup, Grandma's Help, Facebook." *NPR*. Accessed November 28, 2017. www.npr.org/sections/goatsandsoda/2017/07/14/535817998 /what-moms-need-to-breast-feed-chicken-soup-grandmas-help -facebook

Goldman, A. S. "The Immune System in Human Milk and the Developing Infant." *Breastfeeding Medicine* 2, no. 4 (December 2007): 195–204. www.ncbi.nlm.nih.gov/pubmed/18081456

Heacock, H. J. "Influence of Breast vs. Formula Milk in Physiologic Gastroesophageal Reflux in Healthy Newborn Infants." *Journal of Pediatric Gastroenterology and Nutrition* 14, no. 1 (January 1992): 41–46.

Healthcare.gov. "Breastfeeding Benefits." Accessed November 28, 2017. www.healthcare.gov/coverage/breast-feeding-benefits/

Healthychildren.org. "Facts for Fathers about Breastfeeding." Accessed November 28, 2017. www.healthychildren.org/English /ages-stages/baby/breastfeeding/Pages/Facts-for-Fathers-About -Breastfeeding.aspx

International Doula Institute. "Boob, Bottle, or Both: Why Non-judgmental Support Is an Essential Part of Doula Certification." Accessed November 28, 2017. internationaldoulainstitute .com/2016/08/boob-bottle-or-both/

Johnson-Grass, Amy. "15 Cool Facts about Breastfeeding." *Health Foundations Blog*. March 23, 2015. www.health-foundations.com /blog/2013/11/19/15-cool-facts-about-breastfeeding

Kam, Renee. "Montgomery Glands: 7 Interesting Facts." *BellyBelly*. Accessed November 28, 2017. www.bellybelly.com.au/pregnancy /montgomery-glands/

Kendall-Tackett, Kathleen. "Antidepressant Use in Pregnant and Breastfeeding Women." *UppityScienceChick.com*. Accessed November 28, 2017. www.uppitysciencechick.com /antidepressant_use_in_preg.pdf

Lauwers, Judith, and Anna Swisher. *Counseling the Nursing Mother*. 4th ed. Burlington, MA: Jones & Bartlett Learning, 2005.

Murtagh, Lindsey, and Anthony D. Moulton, "Working Mothers, Breastfeeding, and the Law." *American Journal of Public Health* 101, no. 2 (February 2011): 217–23. doi:10.2105/AJPH.2009.185280

Northern Star. "Ryan Reynolds Says Daughter Is 'Totally Average.'" February 6, 2015. https://www.northernstar.com.au/news /ryan-reynolds-says-daughter-totally-average/2535811/

Office on Women's Health. "Incredible Facts about Babies, Breastmilk and Breastfeeding." *Womenshealth.gov*. Accessed November 28, 2017. www.womenshealth.gov/itsonlynatural /addressing-myths/incredible-facts-about-babies-breast-milk.html

People Babies (blog). "The Year in Celebrity Breastfeeding." December 24, 2007. celebritybabies.people.com/2007/12/24 /breastfeeders-0/

San Diego Breastfeeding Center. "How Long Does My Breast Milk Stay Fresh?" Accessed November 28, 2017. www.sdbfc.com /blog/2012/9/12/how-long-does-my-breast-milk-stay-fresh.html

Satter, Ellyn. *Child of Mine: Feeding with Love and Good Sense*. Rev. ed. Boulder, CO: Bull, 2000.

The Second 9 Months (blog). "Lactation Consultant: What Does That Mean?" Accessed November 28, 2017. www.second9months.com /what-does-that-mean/

UNICEF. "Improving Breastfeeding, Complementary Foods and Feeding Practices." Accessed December 11, 2017. www.unicef.org /nutrition/index_breastfeeding.html

US Department of Labor. "FAQs about Affordable Care Act Implementation (Part XXIX) and Mental Health Parity Implementation." Accessed November 28, 2017. www.dol.gov/sites/default/files/ebsa /about-ebsa/our-activities/resource-center/faqs/aca-part-xxix.pdf

Walker, Marsha. *Breastfeeding Management for the Clinician.* 4th ed. Burlington, MA: Jones & Bartlett Learning, 2017.

"Weaning from the Breast." *Paediatrics & Child Health* 9, no. 4 (April 2004): 249–53. www.ncbi.nlm.nih.gov/pmc/articles/PMC2720507/

West, Diana. *Defining Your Own Success: Breastfeeding after Breast Reduction Surgery.* Schaumburg, IL: La Leche League International, 2001.

West, Diana, and Lisa Marasco. *The Breastfeeding Mother's Guide to Making More Milk.* New York: McGraw-Hill, 2009.

Wiessinger, Diane, Diana West, and Teresa Pitman. *The Womanly Art of Breastfeeding.* 8th ed. New York: Ballantine Books, 2010.

Wiessinger, Diane, Diana West, Linda J. Smith, and Teresa Pitman. *Sweet Sleep.* New York: Ballantine Books, 2014.

World Health Organization. "Breastfeeding." Accessed November 28, 2017. www.who.int/maternal_child_adolescent/topics/child /nutrition/breastfeeding/en/

World Health Organization. "Exclusive Breastfeeding." Accessed November 28, 2017. www.who.int/nutrition/topics /exclusive_breastfeeding/en/

Index

Mom stories
  breastfeeding support
    (Stephanie), 17
  inability to breastfeed
    (Elizabeth), 127
  increasing production
    (Natalie), 123–124
  nursing in public (Annaliese), 75
  pumping (Cinda), 91
  skin-to-skin contact (Dawn), 28
  supplementation (Aran), 121–122
  supplementation (Cara), 125
  support (Michelle), 125–126
  tongue ties (Rena), 122–123
  twins (Galit), 124
Montgomery glands, 4, 133
Multiples, 23, 40–42

N

Neonatal hypoglycemia, 31
Night weaning, 111–112
Nipple confusion, 46
Nipple cream, 18, 51–52
Nipples
  and flange size, 71–72
  flat, 57
  and improper latch, 12
  milk blisters, 77
  sore or cracked, 51–52, 76
  tenderness in, 7, 51
Nipple shields, 52
Nursing. *See* Breastfeeding
Nursing bras, 18
Nursing covers, 19
Nursing pads, 18
Nursing tanks, 18
Nutrition
  before delivery, 21

eating to support
  breastfeeding, 54–55
ensuring good, 64–65
lactogenic foods, 63

O

Obesity, 3
Oral development, 3
Oversupply, 82
Oxytocin, 3, 4, 133

P

Paced bottle-feeding, 78, 133
Pacifiers, 46
Pain, nipple, 7, 12, 51–52, 76, 77
Partners, 14
Pediatricians, 15
Plugged ducts, 76, 112, 133
Poop color, 82
Positions
  cradle hold, 35
  cross-cradle hold, 36
  football/clutch hold, 37
  laid-back hold , 34
  side-lying hold, 38
  tandem nursing, 40–42
Postpartum doulas, 22
Pregnancy, 117
Prenatal breastfeeding classes, 22
Prenatal vitamins, 21, 65
Prescription drugs, 23, 63, 76–77
Preterm babies (preemies), 39
Probiotics, 76
Professionals, 16, 20–22
Progesterone, 8, 117
Prolactin, 8, 62, 133
Pumping, 44–45, 63, 69, 87–93, 96–99
Pumps, 19, 70–72

Acknowledgments

This book was truly a community effort, as there is no way I could have had the knowledge to write it (and finish it on time) without the support and assistance of my family, friends, colleagues, and community.

To the mothers who contributed their breastfeeding memoirs for this book: Your bravery to share your honest, raw stories with the world is awe-inspiring, as is your determination to persevere through significant breastfeeding challenges. I feel honored to know you.

To the San Diego Breastfeeding Center families: You are the reason I do what I do. For the past eight years, you have welcomed me into your lives and trusted me with your most precious gift, your children. You inspire me on a daily basis. Your children are so fortunate to have you as their parents. I hope I can continue to support you for many years to come.

To the San Diego Breastfeeding Center staff: What a team we have! Thank you for taking on extra hours and being flexible with scheduling, and for your encouragement during this writing process. I am so grateful for you all!

To Francesca Orlando and Lindsay Stenovec: You both are such brilliant nutritionists. Thank you for your guidance on the nutrition sections! And a special thank-you to Francesca for cleaning up my diet to support my immune system during stressful times!

To Rachel Rothman: Thank you for all of your guidance on introducing solids. You are an incredible nutrition resource for our local families!

To Dawn Dickerson: Thank you for being a compassionate friend and colleague. I really appreciate your guidance with the hospital exam questions as well as always being available to chat about difficult clinical situations.

To Stacy Wagner-Kinnear and Patty Consolazio: You seriously are the best editors I could have ever asked for! You have been so kind, complimentary, and full of intelligent ideas. Stacy, I'm sure your colleagues will miss our illustration conversations, and I hope to collaborate on another book in the near future!

To Ashley Treadwell: My dear friend and first SDBFC colleague. You set the bar high, girl, for the quality of care we should provide to our breastfeeding families. Thank you for encouraging me to write this book, even when I was scared to death!

To Michelle LaPlante, Anney Hall, and Ashley Treadwell (again): The three of you are my rocks, my sages, my cheerleaders, and my continued emotional support. Life wouldn't be nearly as sweet without you. Over 20 years of friendship truly makes a difference!

To Jason Kaplan: Thank you for being an incredible dad to our boys and for encouraging me to start this new career 10 years ago. Without your support, the San Diego Breastfeeding Center wouldn't exist, and I am eternally grateful.

To my parents (Jack, Jeanne, Jennifer, and John): Thank you for being my biggest fans and supporters. You've always taught me to set my goals high and reach for the stars, while helping me stay centered and grounded. There is no way I could have found enough time to write without you picking up my kids each week and without your delicious dinners. Thank you from the bottom of my heart!

To Donovan Roberts: There is no one in the world I would rather sit in a coffee shop and write with. Your encouragement, kindness, and connection swept me off my feet this year. Thank you for keeping the house afloat when I was overwhelmed with work and writing so that I always walked into a peaceful home.

To my sons, Ben and Ryan: You are the most important teachers I have ever had. Who knew overcoming breastfeeding challenges with you both would create a future career for me? Thank you for teaching me patience and humbleness, and that no challenge is too big to overcome. Thank you for always asking about this book and how writing was going. It meant so much to know you were proud of me. I love you both more than you will ever know.

About the Author

Robin Kaplan is an International Board-Certified Lactation Consultant (IBCLC), frequent media commentator on the topic of breastfeeding, and founding host of The Boob Group, a podcast about breastfeeding hosted on New Mommy Media. She launched the San Diego Breastfeeding Center (SDBFC) in 2009 and is an established voice in the parenting world for her knowledge about lactation and her commitment to supporting moms without judging them, a keystone of the SDBFC philosophy. In 2016, Robin started the San Diego Breastfeeding Center Foundation, a 501(c)3 nonprofit organization that provides reduced-rate lactation consultations for local low-income families.

Robin offers in-person consultations for families in San Diego and online consultations throughout the world. She also teaches breastfeeding and social media workshops across the United States. She enjoys working with families of all shapes and sizes, and the SDBFC provides coaching to birth mothers, as well as adoptive parents and lesbian partners, by offering education about induced lactation.

Robin lives in San Diego, California, with her two sons, Benjamin and Ryan, and their dog, Ellie. She loves cooking, fermenting, traveling, hiking, going to the beach, and Italian red wines.

Connect with Robin online!
WEBSITE sdbfc.com
FACEBOOK facebook.com/SanDiegoBreastfeedingCenter
INSTAGRAM @san_diego_breastfeeding_center
YOUTUBE DIYBreastfeeding

CPSIA information can be obtained
at www.ICGtesting.com
Printed in the USA
JSHW022226071021
19397JS00002B/3